The Integrity Clause
A new African Identity

OLUTAYO K. OSUNSAN

Copyright © 2021 Olutayo K. Osunsan

All rights reserved.

ISBN: 9798593433985

For those who truly and sincerely aspire for transformational change and greatness beyond self...

CONTENTS

Introduction 9
Africa..15
Integrity 31
Purpose 40
Respect 52
Trustworthiness 59
Fairness...67
Compassion 76
Humility 89
Loyalty 100
Selflessness...106
Enterprising 113
Moral Courage..118
Conclusion..135

"Here's to the crazy ones. The misfits. The rebels. The troublemakers. The round pegs in the square holes. The ones who see things differently. They're not fond of rules. And they have no respect for the status quo. You can quote them, disagree with them, glorify or vilify them. About the only thing you can't do is ignore them. Because they change things. They push the human race forward. And while some may see them as the crazy ones, we see genius. Because the people who are crazy enough to think they can change the world, are the ones who do."

Steve Jobs (Apple Inc.)

THE INTEGRITY CLAUSE

Introduction

> "The tragedy of Africa is that Africans are in the business of canonizing thieves and demonizing its saints."
> **Patrick L. O. Lumumba**

> "...Corruption is something we talk about...It is something that even the corrupt acknowledge it's a bad thing. But the irony and the tragedy at once is that those who engage in corruption love it. The tragedy at once is that those of us who do not engage in it directly accommodate it...Our levels of tolerance for corruption in Africa is amazing..."
> **Patrick L. O. Lumumba**

Having been a lecturer in several universities for several years, one of the most common questions and discussions I have had with students at all levels has to do with why Africa is the way it is. I have observed over the years that this question comes from an honest place and is propelled by the desire to live in a better society. In the eyes of these students, especially among the undergraduates there, is a hunger to make a difference and change the world. The same hunger I had when I was much younger. Over time, I woke up to the reality that I was an insignificant person in a world of more than seven billion, mostly insignificant people. My mindset back then was informed by the fact that despite of my hunger and passion, someone showed up and crushed my drive, and over time little, pieces of my desire to have an impact and make a difference were littered all over the floor.

I realized over time that I had become the dream crusher myself by telling people that they will wake up to reality after life kicks them around like a football. I stopped dreaming, I stopped believing and I stopped caring. Over the years, as my students asked these questions of why Africa is so poor in spite of the natural resources; why corruption is so endemic; why our educational system is so outdated and why our politicians seem to only look out for their own interests, I began to realize that my answer which was informed by my mindset was nowhere close to good enough. As my children grew older, they started to ask me the same questions from the tender age of five. They were asking why those countries in the movies are so "organized". I remember one of my kids asking if those "people" are better than us. In her mind, she could not reconcile the fact that some people have a better quality of life even though based on her childish indicators. I could not tell her, "that is Africa for you," or that they are just movies.

I always ask my students what they think Africa's problem is when they come up with the question, and the answer ranges from colonialism to a corrupt political system. The rebuttal is that all that is a result of our mindsets and I tell them that Africa's biggest problem is the African. The average African is indifferent to the situation on the continent and has even become an apologist for the way things are. Sadly, some students and a lot of people on the continent have been inducted into the idea that going into politics or business and making "sharp" deals by any means necessary is the hallmark of success in Africa. A lot of Africans have the mindset that they need to "eat" their own share of the shady national pie. Africa's problem is the people who believe they have no power and have no ability to make a difference. Evil always thrives when the just remain silent. Africa's problem is the African mindset that has made us believe that is the way things are. Nothing can be done about it. The political class will drive the country into the dust of abject poverty and anybody who is wise should join them or find a better life elsewhere. That mindset is the problem.

Every year thousands of Africans leave the continent with the hope of a better life anywhere else out of Africa. Some strive and thrive to get a better education, jobs and opportunities abroad while others put their very lives at risk to escape the poverty and devastation that is ravaging the continent. These Africans mostly face inhumane conditions; they are trafficked, exploited and face racism amidst other challenges. In spite of it all, many are gladly willing to remain in those dire conditions than return to Africa. Strangely you'll hear in the African media how the economy is growing and the GDP and other economic indicators are painting a "promising" picture, but for the average African these indicators mean nothing. The indicators don't put food on their tables, clothes on their backs and roofs over their heads. The economic growth Africa is experiencing does not afford most Africans the dignity to live a decent life. As the corona-virus pandemic continues to hit the continent, more Africans will grow even more desperate to itch out at the very least a substandard life for their families. They cannot afford to be in lockdown because they live hand to mouth; they cannot afford basic education, not to mention online learning; they cannot even afford family planning. By the time the dust settles after the Covid-19 pandemic, a big chunk of the middle class will be dragged into poverty. Both the urban and rural poor will increase in number and severity.

As I always tell my students, Africa's biggest and most valuable resource is its people. The mindsets of its people will dictate the nature of the families, the communities, the countries and the continent. When Africans wake up to the fact that they are the solutions to the predicament they find themselves in, the continent will truly be transformed. The government institutions cannot do it, the donors cannot do it and the "others" can't do it without you doing your part as an African.

Africans need to wake up to the fact that the history of the world was shaped by Africa and the significant contributions made by Africans may have been suppressed but are still evident. It is important to know that where we are does not indicate who we are and what we can become is not a result of where we have been. Our past can be a motivation to propel us to do and be better.

Despite the fact that history has been whitewashed and African achievements have been erased, my purpose in writing this book is to challenge Africans and young Africans in particular that the future belongs to them. To be an African is not about your skin colour, the language you speak or the country you were born in; it is about the identity you possess in your heart. There are black people who hate Africa and Africans with a passion, while there are whites who love Africa and Africans with a passion. We even have African presidents and government officials who hate their country, countrymen and women. That is why they loot the country and stash all the substances they steal as part of their personal investments in other parts of the world. They hand over the entire economy to "foreign investors" who treat African citizens like slaves. These foreign investors are given incentives and tax holidays, while the African-owned businesses are overtaxed and disenfranchised. To be an African is about the heart and the desire to make Africa a better place. When all is said and done, we are all Africans if we trace our ancestry far back enough. Please note that the intention of this book is not about hate or creating rifts, it is about owning one's own identity and respecting it and that of others. It is about the frank and honest truth and trying to deal with reality. It is about what I believe can be done in my own little way.

Africa needs people who have integrity, people who think beyond themselves and people who want to create a better society for all Africans. This calls for a personal decision, a paradigm shift and a mind shift that will birth the right mindset. A mindset that will see the good and the potential that the continent holds. This book is for those who want to give it a try and make a difference. To those who want to do something about it. This book is for those who have made the resolve that Africa can be a better place for posterity. This book is the call to activate the integrity clause.

Olutayo K. Osunsan

Africa

"A people denied history is a people deprived of dignity."
Ali A. Mazrui

"Africa PRODUCES what it does NOT CONSUME and CONSUMES what it does NOT PRODUCE."
Ali A. Mazrui

"You don't necessarily need atomic bombs to destroy a nation. Politicians who value their pockets than the life of citizens always do that every day."
Israelmore Ayivor

"Development is about more than money, or machines, or good

policies- it's about real people and
the lives they lead."
Paul Kagame

They say history is written by the victors. In the last few centuries, Africa and Africans have been vanquished. Enslaved, looted, colonized, marginalized and recolonised; our recent history as Africans is no longer our own. In fact, nothing is ours anymore; not even our names. African countries bear names given by others and some of the citizens answer to names not indigenous to Africa. Our history has been rewritten by the victors and we are the hopeless, mindless, uncivilized villains in it. It suggests that our identity is evil and our continent is dark; and only the light of the civilized victors can help us overcome our darkness[1]. Africans are taught about the white saviours in school: they discovered our countries; we are named after them and our elites want to be like them. We as Africans have been programmed to believe that our salvation and ultimate success can only be found in the bosoms of our colonisers; the victors. Africans have been taught to hate themselves and their type and favour the perceived white saviours.[2]

African history is a tragic story. The story of a people whose identity is soiled and villainized. To be black is to

---

[1]Olusoga, D. (2016, May 10). The roots of European racism lie in the slave trade, colonialism- and Edward Long | David Olusoga. The Guardian. https://www.theguardian.com/commentisfree/2015/sep/08/european-racism-africa-slavery
[2]Khalifa, M. (2015). Can Blacks be racists? Black-on-Black principal abuse in an urban school setting. International Journal of Qualitative Studies in Education, 28(2), 259-282.

be less. To be black is to be less than an equal. The mass murder of Africans through history is always relegated to the past. Africans and their descendants are assured the world has changed and the disregard for African lives is no longer a thing.[3] Sadly, even in 2022, it continues to be confirmed that Africans and their descendants in the diaspora are second-class humans[4]. Institutionalized racism, geopolitical dynamics and systematic suppression of Africans and those with African ancestry are very prevalent.[5]

Both the Covid-19 pandemic[6] and the global outcry concerning the war in Ukraine[7] confirm the lesser place that Africa holds in human society. While other parts of the western world are getting their second and third booster shots, several Africans are yet to get vaccinated. If not for divine providence, the pandemic would have ravaged African nations. African nations have been invaded and leaders have been forcefully removed and even murdered without due process[8]. The claim is that democracy has won and the said nation has been "liberated". The same happens to a European nation and

---

[3] Michael, L. (2015). Afrophobia in Ireland: Racism against people of African descent. Dublin: ENAR Ireland
[4] Elshabazz-Palmer, A. (2017). Scientific Racism: The Exploitation of African Americans. Intertext, 25(1), 10.
[5] BBC News. (2018, November 28). Racism widespread across Europe, study says. https://www.bbc.com/news/world-europe-46369046
[6] Tilley, H. (2020). COVID-19 across Africa: colonial hangovers, racial hierarchies, and medical histories. Journal of West African History, 6(2), 155-179.
[7] Al Jazeera (2022). 'Double standards': Western coverage of Ukraine war criticised. (2022). Retrieved 9 March 2022, from https://www.aljazeera.com/news/2022/2/27/western-media-coverage-ukraine-russia-invasion-criticism
[8] Green, M. (2019). To What Extent Was the NATO Intervention in Libya a Humanitarian Intervention. E-International Relations Students, 1-4.

there is an outcry and outright rejection from western nations, media channels and every other institution. Through it all, some Africans in Ukraine were even denied access to safety in the neighbouring countries[9]. All loss of life is unacceptable in any conflict, but it appears the loss of black lives is acceptable when the need arises. To be black on this earth is a disadvantage; to be African is a burden; and to be a black African and poor is a life sentence of misery, lack and insignificance. Truly, there is no country for a black man or woman because even in their own countries, they don't really matter unless they are part of the ruling elite or the wealthy. Africans do not stand on an equal footing as others, not because they were born unequal, but because they were born in a depressed geography of history. Black people everywhere are more likely to be victims of racism than any other race on the planet,[10] even in their own countries.

The truth is that we are all part of one race; the human race. In reality, we are all Africans and the whole concept of race is simply a social-political construction that our society has developed to put people in categories. These categories make it easy for one to take advantage of the other. One race to conquer, subdue, colonize and exploit the others. To be African or from Africa places you in a

---

[9]Tovey, M. (2022). African refugees fleeing Ukraine are facing 'shocking' racism. Retrieved 9 March 2022, from https://www.dailymail.co.uk/news/article-10562031/African-refugees-fleeing-Ukraine-facing-shocking-racism-Nigerians-told-no-blacks-bus.html
[10]Sule, A. O. (2019, August 12). Racism harms black people most. It's time to recognise "anti-blackness." The Guardian. https://www.theguardian.com/commentisfree/2019/aug/09/black-people-racism-anti-blackness-discrimination-minorities

category that can easily be undermined. For most of modern history, Africa has been the bottom of the barrel. It is seen as a backward place and it was labelled "the Dark Continent" that needed to be explored and discovered[11]. The same Africa that birthed great civilizations and empires that span centuries. In case you are not familiar with some of these civilizations, let's look at a few.

Kingdom of Kush
The kingdom of Kush which was located in Sudan was lavished with ivory, incense, iron and gold. This ancient Nubian empire reached its peak in the second millennium B.C.; they were military rivals of the Egyptians and even ruled Egypt as the 25th Dynasty. In spite of most people knowing only about the Egyptian pyramids, the ancient Kushite capital of Meroe is home to the ruins of over 200 pyramids.

The Punts
The land of the Punt was located by the Red Sea coast of East Africa which was referred to as "the land of the gods" over flowing with ebony, gold, myrrh and exotic animals by the Egyptians. Egypt was headed in the 15th century B.C. by Queen Hatshepsut, who was the longest-reigning female pharaoh. She ruled for 20 years and was considered one of Egypt's most successful pharaohs[12]. Her famous trade expeditions in

---

[11]Thompsell, A. (2019, July 2). *Why was Africa called the Dark Continent?* ThoughtCo. https://www.thoughtco.com/why-africa-called-the-dark-continent-43310
[12]Andrews, E. (2018, August 22). *7 Influential African Empires*. HISTORY.

1493 BC to the Punt in the 18th Dynasty of Egypt were well documented. Queen Hatshepsut claimed that her divine mother, the Egyptian goddess Hathor, was from Punt and other inscriptions indicate that Egyptians in the 18th Dynasty considered Punt the origin of their culture[13].

Carthage

Carthage was located to the north of Africa in modern-day Tunisia and was a rival of Rome in the Punic Wars. Carthage's influence eventually extended from North Africa to Spain and parts of the Mediterranean into the Atlantic, and across the Sahara Desert. Boasting of one of the largest military forces in the ancient world, Carthage attacked Rome twice, and on both occasions, almost destroyed Rome. The Third Punic war led to its destruction by the Romans after a heavy siege. Hannibal Barca a Carthaginian general and statesman who commanded Carthage's main army against Rome during the Second Punic War (218–201 BC) was widely considered as one of the greatest military commanders in the world's history.

Aksum Empire

The Empire of Aksum(or Axum)held sway over parts of what is now Eritrea and northern Ethiopia[14]. The empire spanned modern-day Ethiopia, Eritrea, Djibouti, Egypt, Saudi Arabia, Somalia, South Sudan,

---

https://www.history.com/news/7-influential-african-empires
[13]Creasman, P. P. (2014). Hatshepsut and the Politics of Punt. African Archaeological Review, 31(3), 395-405.
[14]Andrews, E. (2018, August 22). *7 Influential African Empires*. HISTORY. https://www.history.com/news/7-influential-african-empires

Sudan, and Yemen[15]. The empire of Aksum is notable for a number of achievements, such as its own alphabet; the Ge'ez alphabet, and it also developed a distinctive architectural style that involved the building of massive stone obelisks. Aksum was deeply involved in the trade network between India and the Mediterranean (Rome, later Byzantium), exporting ivory, tortoise shells, gold and emeralds, and importing silk and spices. Aksum became one of the first empires in the world to adopt Christianity, which led to a political and military alliance with the Byzantines. According to Ethiopian tradition, the queen of Sheba returned to her capital, Aksum, in northern Ethiopia, and months later gave birth to Solomon's son, who is named Menelik, meaning "Son of the Wise".[16]

Mali Empire
In West Africa, Sundiata Keita, also known as the "Lion King"—led a revolt against a Sosso king and united his subjects into a new state that established the Mali Empire which dates to the 1200s. This empire spanned a big part of West Africa including modern-day Gambia, Guinea, Guinea-Bissau, Ivory Coast, Mali, Mauritania, Niger, and Senegal. It spawned important cities such as Djenné, Gao and Timbuktu. It became renowned for the wealth of its rulers; especially Musa Keita believed to be the wealthiest person in the Middle Ages and possibly in history. Musa

---

[15]Toit, M. (2020, March 5). *9 Ancient African Kingdoms You Should Know About.* Rhino Africa Blog. https://blog.rhinoafrica.com/2018/03/27/9-ancient-african-kingdoms/
[16]Wood, M. (2011, February 17). *BBC - History - Ancient History in depth: The Queen of Sheba.* BBC. http://www.bbc.co.uk/history/ancient/cultures/sheba_01.shtml

ascended the throne of the Mali Empire in 1312 after Abu-Bakr II, his predecessor who he deputized went missing on a voyage to find the edge of the Atlantic Ocean. It is believed that Musa Keita's trip to Mecca caused a stir when he passed through Egypt with his entourage of tens of thousands of people, livestock and gold[17]. While in Cairo, he reluctantly met the Sultan of Cairo and his generosity made the price of gold drop in Egypt for the next 12 years. His name and story spread across the known world. The Mali Empire was the largest empire in West Africa and profoundly influenced the culture of West Africa through the spread of its language, laws and customs. This golden age of Mali enhanced sub-Saharan Trade and increased its spread across Europe and Asia Minor. Musa Keita is also remembered for his faith in Islam, advancement of education, and patronage of culture in Mali[18].

The Great Zimbabwe

The Great Zimbabwe covered a large chunk of modern-day Botswana, Zimbabwe and Mozambique. It was particularly rich in cattle and precious metals, and stood across a trade route that connected the region's gold fields with ports on the Indian Ocean coast. Though little is known about its history, the remains of artifacts such as Chinese pottery, Arabian glass and European textiles indicate that it was once a well-connected

---

[17]Hughes, T. (2019, June 11). *10 Facts About Mansa Musa – Richest Man in History?* History Hit. https://www.historyhit.com/facts-about-mansa-musa-richest-man-in-history/
[18]National Geographic Society. (2020, March 4). *Mansa Musa (Musa I of Mali)*. https://www.nationalgeographic.org/encyclopedia/mansa-musa-musa-i-mali/

mercantile center. This civilization had a monopoly on the trade of gold and ivory from the southeastern coast of the continent to the interior and were famed miners specializing in minerals such as copper, iron, and gold. The majority of scholars believe that it was built by members of the Gokomere culture, who were ancestors of modern Shona in Zimbabwe.

Many other kingdoms and empires existed including, The Kingdom of Ghana (also known as Wagadu), the Songhai Empire, The Kingdom of Mutapa, The Kingdom of Kongo, and The Benin Empire, to mention but a few[19]. Sadly, these heritages are not as willingly taught in African schools.

Over the years, with no regard to their rich history, African people were labelled as savages and treated like the beasts of the fields. The culture was termed primitive and needed to be educated and civilized.[20] Africa was looted and ravaged for centuries and when the Africans spoke for independence it was resisted. Africans cannot govern themselves and to prove this, our "colonial masters" sowed seeds of division as they granted their African colonies independence. African leaders with aspirations to make the continent great rose and they became one with an African identity and the need for unity. The colonial powers stood behind the veil of well-wishers as they pulled the strings that exacerbated chaos,

---

[19]Toit, M. (2020, March 5). *9 Ancient African Kingdoms You Should Know About.* Rhino Africa Blog. https://blog.rhinoafrica.com/2018/03/27/9-ancient-african-kingdoms/

[20]Thompsell, A. (2019, July 2). *Why was Africa called the Dark Continent?* ThoughtCo. https://www.thoughtco.com/why-africa-called-the-dark-continent-43310

and as civil wars and political unrest brewed, weapons that Africans don't produce flooded the continent. Poverty stripped the continent of its dignity and political leaders with slave-mentalities went back to eat from the palms of their former masters. Neo-colonization is now dressed as international trading partners coming under the guise of mutual trade[21]. Of course, this might appear extreme, but a part of the unrest in Africa can be attributed to the people who provide the weapons and the unrealistic loans that keep African countries in chains.

As Bishop Desmond Tutu placed it, "when the missionaries came to Africa, they had the Bible and we had the land. They said, "let us pray." We closed our eyes. When we opened them, we had the Bible and they had the land." The Europeans brought religion and claimed they discovered Africa in spite of the fact that everything the Europeans discovered in Africa was shown to them by the natives. Strangely, some will argue that both Christianity and Islam were already on the African continent even before the missionaries arrived[22]. This is confirmed by the fact that several Africans and African civilisations were mentioned in the bible, even before Christianity got to Europe. "Discovered" African landmarks are given European names from Nalubaale to Lake Victoria; from Eko to Lagos; from Mosi-oa-Tunya to Victoria Falls. The continent of Africa is sprinkled with European names from nations to streets. African

---

[21]Rodney, W. (2018). How europe underdeveloped africa. Verso Books.
[22]BBC World Service. (n.d.). *The Story of Africa*. BBC. Retrieved July 4, 2020, from
https://www.bbc.co.uk/worldservice/africa/features/storyofafrica/index_section8.shtml

students are taught that their countries were discovered by white men and the wiser teachers say the "first white man". Our education equates good English with intelligence and academic acumen. We are told to speak English or French and our native languages are discouraged at school. It is a proven fact that students learn better in their native tongue[23]. African languages are dying out and we have modern-day African youths who can't speak or write in their mother tongue[24]. They are instead praised for their command of the English language or ridiculed for their heavy African accents.

Africa's story is a tragic one and it is painted by the fact that for a big part of history, Africans have been told they are not good enough. Africans have been treated as second-class citizens, even in their very own country, continent and on the planet. African accomplishments and history have been edited, and in some cases, deleted from history, and the ones that remain have been white-washed. Proof of this is the fact that when you watch Hollywood movies about ancient Egypt, for example, the Egyptians are white. Some even claim that ancient Egyptians are not white nor are they black. However, documented historical evidence indicates that the Sphinx have been described as having Nubian or sub-Saharan features. And from historic text, Greek authors like Herodotus and Aristotle referred to Egyptians as having

---

[23]Kioko, A. (2015, January 16). Why schools should teach young learners in home language | British Council. British Council.
https://www.britishcouncil.org/voices-magazine/why-schools-should-teach-young-learners-home-language
[24]Mberia, W. (2014). Kithaka. "Death and Survival of African Languages in the 21st Century.". International Journal of Linguistics and Communication, 2(3), 127-44.

dark skin[25].

Another example of African achievement being deleted from history is the fact that African travelers set foot in the Americas even before Christopher Columbus. This fact was documented by Christopher Columbus himself and other explorers such as Vasco Nunez de Balboa. African artifacts and even skeletons are being found to corroborate the fact that Africans helped civilize America way before Europeans "discovered" it[26]. This was way before Europeans claim to have discovered and civilized Africa. Africans did not go to the Americas to colonize or civilize them; they went there to learn more and exchange cultures[27].

One of the first documented pieces of evidence of Africans navigating the seas to settling in the Americas were black Egyptians headed by King Ramses III of the 19th dynasty in 1292 BC. This was corroborated by the Greek historian, Herodotus, who wrote about how Ancient Egyptian pharaohs were prolific sailors and navigators[28]. Similarly, the Malians, inspired by King

---

[25]Abad-Santos, A. (2014, August 4). *Hollywood likes to pretend that ancient Egypt was full of white people*. Vox.
https://www.vox.com/2014/8/4/5955253/Hollywood-egypt-white-people-exodus-gods-and-kings
[26]Waweru, N. (2018, August 10). *Here's proof that Africans settled in South America long before Columbus's voyage*. Face2Face Africa.
https://face2faceafrica.com/article/heres-proof-that-africans-settled-in-south-america-long-before-columbus-started-his-voyage
[27]Chengu, G. (2018, October 8). *Before Columbus: How Africans Brought Civilization to America*. TRANSCEND Media Service.
https://www.transcend.org/tms/2018/10/before-columbus-how-africans-brought-civilization-to-america/#:%7E:text=One%20of%20the%20first%20documented,great%20seafaring%20and%20navigational%20skills.

Abubakari II the predecessor of Mansa Musa, made the trip in 1300 sending out 200 ships of men, and 200 ships of trade material, crops, animals, and cloth, and importantly exporting African knowledge of astronomy, religion and the arts.[29] This is further confirmed by the fact that archaeologists have found several artifacts that substantiate that Africans had "discovered" and lived in South America as far back as 13,000 BC to 600 AD. The evidence indicates that people from Axum, Meroe and the Land of Punt began settling in South America between this time, according to the remains found in archeological dig projects in Ecuador, Valdivia, Chile, and among the Ponuencho of Peru[30].

Most importantly, African societies were following their own patterns of development before the onset of European intervention. Sadly, early Euro-American historians could not live with the fact that Africans had contributed to the fabric and cultural identity of the Americas way before the transatlantic slave trade began in the 13th century. This kills the notion that Africans were inferior and the only thing for them to do was to rewrite history by erasing the African contribution[31].

---

[28]Kphera, S. (2001, January). *"They Came before Columbus". (Cover Story/Africans in the Americas)*. New African.
https://www.questia.com/magazine/1G1-82064376/they-came-before-columbus-cover-story-africans
[29]Baxter, J. (2000, December 13). BBC News | AFRICA | Africa's "greatest explorer." BBC News. http://news.bbc.co.uk/2/hi/africa/1068950.stm
[30]Waweru, N. (2018, August 10). *Here's proof that Africans settled in South America long before Columbus's voyage*. Face2Face Africa.
https://face2faceafrica.com/article/heres-proof-that-africans-settled-in-south-america-long-before-columbus-started-his-voyage
[31]Kphera, S. (2001, January). *"They Came before Columbus". (Cover Story/Africans in the Americas)*. New African.

Africans were denied their history and stripped of their dignity. We were made to believe that the white man is our salvation; that God is white and the devil is black. Africans were made to believe that freedom is a privilege and not a fundamental right. By the 18th century Scottish philosopher, David Hume, suggested: "I am apt to suspect the Negroes to be naturally inferior to the Whites. There scarcely ever was a civilized nation of that complexion, nor even any individual, eminent either in action or in speculation. No ingenious manufacture among them, no arts, no sciences."[32] In the 19th century, the German philosopher, Hegel, simply remarked that Africa "is no historical part of the world; it has no movement or development to exhibit." Africa was deemed illiterate, uncivilized, ungoverned, unshaped, a place of dark chaos. Some Africans now believe Africa is bad and foreign is good; from products, to education to identity. To be associated with the foreign is more sophisticated than being associated with the African identity. From hot red lipsticks and weaves to faked accents and skin bleaching; some Africans want to totally rid themselves of their identity.

As stated by John Henrik Clarke, "the cruelest thing slavery and colonialism did to the Africans was to destroy their memory of what they were before foreign contact", this statement could not be truer. Africa has been perceived and portrayed by the media as a bowl of hopelessness and destitution. In the worlds' collective

---

https://www.questia.com/magazine/1G1-82064376/they-came-before-columbus-cover-story-africans

[32] Eze, E. C. (2000). Hume, race, and human nature. *Journal of the History of Ideas, 61*(4), 691-698.

conciseness, Africa has always been poor and needy. Marcus Garvey emphasized that: "A people without the knowledge of their past history, origin and culture is like a tree without roots". Without roots, how can one be planted and stand firm? It is a fact that Bernie Grant pointed out: "The colonization and exploitation of Africa and the enslavement of African people must be the biggest crime in the whole of history, and one from which we still suffer, both materially and psychologically." Through recent history, Africans have been mistreated and undermined both at home and abroad. They are pounded with the information that Africans are lazy, dirty and disease-riddled, and that Africans lack the intellectual ability to thrive. A big part of the African collective memory is still in shackles and needs emancipation from mental slavery as Bob Marley sang.

This was made worse by contemporary Africa being burdened with leadership and governance problems. We have people with no sense of duty taking up leadership positions, people who see politics and governance as a business or a drive to loot. We have countries that export crude oil and import petroleum[33]; we have presidents who have failed to accept the voice of the people[34]; we have individuals who run the country like their personal investments[35]; and we have unprecedented levels of

---

[33]BALA-GBOGBO, E. (2019, October 21). *Africa's biggest crude producer remains stuck on imported fuels*. World Oil. https://www.worldoil.com/news/2019/10/21/africa-s-biggest-crude-producer-remains-stuck-on-imported-fuels
[34]Adejumobi, S. (2000). Elections in Africa: A fading shadow of democracy? *International Political Science Review, 21*(1), 59-73.
[35]Arun, N. (2019, July 15). *Zuma, the Guptas, and the sale of South Africa*. BBC

corruption[36]. All this makes it hard to believe that Africa was a great continent with a remarkable heritage and leaders who sought to do exceptional things. Every day, the average African is forced to try to make sense of everyday life. The institutions are failing and where they work, they seem to only work for the privileged few. It is almost tempting sometimes for a frustrated African to agree with the racist philosophers.

All is not lost: this chapter is solely to point out the fact that Africa is not as hopeless as it appears; that Africans have been there and done that before. This chapter is to point out what has been done and what can be done when people choose to follow their own destiny. This chapter is to point out that it is only Africans who can help Africa. Africa does not need another political system; it does not need more donor funds or more talent. Africa needs people who are determined to make a difference in spite of all that is said about Africa and all that is happening. Africa needs people who will prove that Africa is not an illiterate, uncivilized, ungoverned, unshaped place of dark chaos. Africa needs leaders and citizens who are ready to serve a purpose greater than themselves; a purpose to transform the continent for posterity. Africa needs more Africans with integrity.

News. https://www.bbc.com/news/world-africa-48980964
[36]Transparency International. (2020, June 12). *Citizens speak out about corruption in Africa - News*. Transparency.Org. https://www.transparency.org/en/news/citizens-speak-out-about-corruption-in-africa

THE INTEGRITY CLAUSE

Integrity

> "The greatness of a man is not in how much wealth he acquires, but in his integrity and ability to affect those around him positively."
> **Bob Marley**

> "There is no higher value in our society than integrity."
> **Arlen Specter**

> "One of the truest tests of integrity is its blunt refusal to be compromised"
> **Chinua Achebe**

It is a common fact that talent, ability and hard work can lift a person to exceptional heights, but the absence of character; the absence of integrity will guarantee that the individual does not remain at such lofty heights. Integrity is an anchor that protects people who possess it. Integrity is the foundation on which lasting societies are built. The single highest significant quality you can ever develop that will augment every part of your life is the value of integrity[37]. Integrity is the essential ingredient to a successful and happy life. Integrity is attributed to numerous aspects of an individual's life. They include those qualities such as professional, intellectual and artistic integrity.

- Professional integrity is preserving proper ethical behavior. It is the habit of exhibiting consistent observance to ethical and moral values and standards such as honesty, respect, reliability and dependability. In other words, doing your job with utmost professionalism.
- Intellectual integrity is the determination to be exhaustive and honest to acquire the truth or to reach the most authentic decision in a given situation. A person with intellectual integrity is driven by the desire to be logical, follow reasons and evidence boldly anywhere they may lead in an attempt to find the truth. In other words, don't just believe what people tell you, draw your own conclusions.
- Artistic integrity is commonly the aptitude to neglect a tolerable level of contrasting, disrupting, and corrupting values that could otherwise alter an artist's or entities' authentic vision in a way that

---

[37]Essays, UK. (November 2018). The Importance of Integrity in Society Philosophy Essay. Retrieved from https://www.ukessays.com/essays/philosophy/the-importance-of-integrity-in-society-philosophy-essay.php?vref=1

disrupts their own defined artistic ideals and personal values. In other words, being true to self.

Integrity is more than ethics and ethical standards at the individual level. It is all about the character of the individual. It is those characteristics of an individual that are constantly thoughtful, empathetic, transparent, truthful, and moral. Integrity is acting in agreement or concord with pertinent moral values, norms, and rules. Integrity means following your moral or ethical principles and doing the right thing in all situations. The essence of integrity is about doing the right thing even when it's not recognized by others, or suitable for you. Having integrity suggests you are true to yourself and what you morally stand for. It means you would do nothing that demeans or dishonours you. Trust, honour, and honesty are key elements to the concept of integrity. Integrity is the solid foundation of good character. A person who has integrity also has an untarnished character and strives to do right in every area of his or her life. It is a fact that integrity helps to develop character.

Integrity is argued to be the most important trait of leadership[38] in any society since irrespective of what other valuable characteristics exist, people will not follow a leader unless they have established trust with him or her. The trust is created through the leader's character which is a result of integrity. In organizations,

---

[38] Mintz, S. (2013, February 20). *Integrity: The most Important Trait of Leadership*. Workplace Ethics Advice.
https://www.workplaceethicsadvice.com/2013/02/integrity-the-most-important-trait-of-leadership-.html

employees who act with integrity will always tell the truth, are accountable and reliable, and treat coworkers, stakeholders and customers with respect. In governance, integrity is a crucial element of trust. Studies have proposed the link between trust in politicians, both from the business fraternity and citizens as a whole, and the perception of corruption[39]. Trust is the result of integrity. There is a relationship between good leadership, accountability, and integrity.

If you have lived in Africa long enough, integrity might not be the first thing to come to mind. There is a serious lack of integrity on the continent. We have the famous "African time" which shows no regard for time keeping and even encourages tardiness as a sign of being busy or hardworking. It is not uncommon for a guest of honour to arrive two to three hours late and give the excuse of being held up in a meeting. This excuse only shows that the person is not organized and has no respect for the people who invited him or her. On the other extreme, we have politicians who promise heaven and earth with the full knowledge that they will not deliver. In fact, to have integrity in Africa is to be someone that society might frown on because people at times like shortcuts and "technical know who". If you go by the books, people will say you are bad and you lack compassion. To be compassionate is to break the rules and manipulate the system for the people you know. That is the mindset. To get a job in an organization, you might be asked "who sent you?" or "who do you know?", these types of questions at job interviews show that your qualifications

---

[39] OECD. (n.d.). *Trust in Government - Integrity and fairness - OECD*. Retrieved July 10, 2020, from http://www.oecd.org/gov/trust-integrity-and-fairness.htm

or experience has nothing to do with the job. This is very much the case with government jobs. It is not uncommon for the average citizen to beg a Police Officer to take a bribe instead of enforcing the law. To have integrity is to be a bad person and sometimes your workmates can plot against you. Of course, this does not apply to every African, however, this mindset needs to change. To build a workable law-abiding society where everyone has the opportunity to thrive, integrity has to be the corner stone of every institution from the public to the private sector.

According to Steven Wickham, integrity is rare these days. There are however four ways to identify it in others as we aspire to it ourselves: To show consistency, speak truthfully, act rightly, and accept responsibility.[40] The identifier of individuals who have integrity is, they constantly exert the highest quality of work in everything they do. They are the individuals who are always frank and honest in everything they do. Individuals who have and understand integrity know that everything they do is a statement about who they are as a person. Every time a person compromises with integrity, they disrespect and belittle themselves, and undermine the right thing to do. They tell those who look up to them it is okay to compromise integrity.

Some can argue that integrity has a cultural dimension, but we all know that generally speaking, even our conscience can tell us what is right and what is wrong. *The Golden Rule* is the principle of treating others as you

---

[40]Wickham, S. (2015, July 26). *4 Dimensions of Integrity for a God-Faithful Life*. Epitome. http://epitemnein-epitomic.blogspot.com/2015/07/4-dimensions-of-integrity-for-god.html

want to be treated[41]. It is a maxim that cuts across cultures and religions and it simply calls for integrity. The website, "Power of Positivity"[42] advised on how to have integrity by sharing the traits of people with integrity. These traits include:
1. They choose to do the right thing.
2. They are only interested in doing the right thing.
3. They are willing to help those in need.
4. They are willing to give others the benefit of doubt.
5. They make the effort to be honest in all things.
6. They show respect to everyone regardless of status.
7. They are always humble.
8. They have no problem admitting when they're wrong.
9. They will always fulfill their obligations.
10. They are unrelentingly kind.

This list is a tall order, but for people with true integrity, they try to consistently live by the stated. Human imperfection is not an excuse not to try to be a better person. Integrity is a trait that everyone should strive for.

The necessity for integrity in society can never be overstated.[43] In the past, there was a time when no one

---

[41]Flew, A., ed. (1979). "golden rule". *A Dictionary of Philosophy*. London: Pan Books in association with The MacMillan Press

[42]Power of Positivity. (2020, June 26). *10 Traits of Someone with True Integrity*. Power of Positivity: Positive Thinking & Attitude. https://www.powerofpositivity.com/integrity-traits/

[43]Albrecht, S. W. (2017, September 12). *Why the Lack of Integrity Burdens Society*. Wheatley Institution. https://wheatley.byu.edu/why-lack-of-integrity-burdens-society/

felt there was a need for a written contract. A person's word was all that was required. People's words had value and were trustworthy. Adversaries would settle disputes by accepting verbal terms and conditions from people who, days earlier, were fighting to their death. Business transactions and trade would take place based on a verbal representation and conclude with a handshake. Even today, there are some people and businesses that have so much integrity that they can be trusted with anything. The fact is that they are very few. In the past, it took a whole village to raise a child. Now, you can't even trust your child with the neighbours. There is a lack of integrity and a serious lack of trust.

Integrity is not just being true to our convictions. Rather, it is "believing and doing what is true." In order to realize the fruits of integrity in families or organizations, integrity must be nurtured from the inside-out. It is mostly a personal choice and drive to operate with integrity. Integrity cannot be forced on a person; it must be self-driven and the only two ways to make that happen is to model the appropriate behaviour and to invest resources in education. Scholars call this technique modeling (being an example) and labeling (teaching and training). There is no outside-in method that will instill integrity. Integrity is a personal choice and there has to be reason enough to choose it. If it is modelled and the fruits are evident in society more will embrace it. Integrity needs to be rewarded in society and not villainized.

This means that parents have a core role to play as role models because they influence a lot in the lives of their children. It also means that the educational system has to adopt a transformative learning approach where values and evolving mindsets are incorporated into learning. Education should not just be about acquiring knowledge. Quality education intends to nurture a balanced set of competencies in learners to enable them to become economically industrious, develop sustainable livelihoods, contribute to an equitable society and improve the wellbeing of others. As Martin Luther King Jr. said, "intelligence plus character – that is the goals of true education". Good quality education should always develop character and establish a person of integrity. We have brilliant chief accountants who are actually thief accountants because they had no sense of duty, morality and integrity. They are willing to steal, misappropriate and misallocate resources with little or no regard for what is right. Graduates need to come to the workplace knowing that integrity is a core competence in their career progression. It means they have to see people with little or no integrity failing and not celebrated as is the current case[44]. If the role models and leaders are people without integrity, don't expect anything different in society from what already is. Integrity is not a luxury of the wealthy, it is a human necessity for a society to survive, develop and thrive[45].

To conclude, it is important to have integrity and ethics in life. Teach your children early in life the importance of

---

[44]Nicholas-Omoregbe, O. S., Kehinde, O. J., Imhonopi, D., & Evbuoma, I. K. (2016). Good governance and leadership: Pathway to sustainable national development in Nigeria. Journal of Public Administration and Governance, 6(1), 35-49.
[45]Nwankwo, O. F. (2014). Impact of corruption on economic growth in Nigeria. Mediterranean Journal of Social Sciences, 5(6), 41.

integrity and choose to be a person of integrity. It will help establish a society that embraces the true value of life. Integrity is the foundation of enduring societies. African society will be totally transformed if we have more people who understand the value of integrity and how it always pays off in the long run.

Purpose

"The purpose of government is to enable the people of a nation to live in safety and happiness. Government exists for the interests of the governed, not for the governors."
Thomas Jefferson

"The purpose of life is not to be happy. It is to be useful, to be honorable, to be compassionate, to have it make some difference that you have lived and lived well."
Ralph Waldo Emerson

"Everyone has a purpose in life…a unique gift or special talent to give to others. And when we blend this unique talent with service to others, we experience the ecstasy and exultation of our own spirit, which is the ultimate goal of goals."

Deepak Chopra

Purpose is very important in life and to the biggest extent, it gives identity, focus, and shapes vision and direction. Purpose makes people prolific and efficient. Even better is a noble purpose, such as changing the destiny of a continent, a nation, a community or even a family. Surely, purpose is different from just making a living. As John F. Kennedy stated "Efforts and courage are not enough without purpose and direction," purpose is deliberate and intended. It is important to know that a sense of purpose not only helps you to find and do things that add meaning to your life but it also helps when things go wrong. It is a reminder as to who you are and what you stand for. A purpose-driven life is important to succeed in anything including life as a whole. A healthy sense of purpose helps you to put those events in perspective, to refocus the things that are meaningful to you, and to move ahead and enjoy life.

Purpose is argued to be the starting point of life; in other words if you don't have a purpose, then you have not or are not living. You need to have something to live for, otherwise what is the purpose of life? Clear purpose in life leads to clear goals and plans which can influence our everyday actions and decisions. This helps us to determine what is and is not important and ultimately results into finding fulfillment in life. In the continent of

Africa, several people don't have a purpose or at the very least they don't know what their purpose is. Most Africans will say they want a good life; they don't want to be poor; they want to educate their children; and maybe buy land and build a home. Sadly, in most African countries, there is no collective purpose and that is why when a new government comes into power, they scrap what the old government was doing and start afresh. In so doing, the country goes around the same "hill" for years. Even in countries where one person has been president for 30 to 40 years; you still find there is no purpose. That is why when that government finally fails, the countries crumble and go into chaos. This is a lack of purpose, focus and shortsightedness at work.

Purpose, as I pointed out earlier, is good, but a purpose greater than one's self is even better; a purpose that is for the greater good. Some of the most amazing countries in the world are countries that look at the long-term aspect of development and growth. They look out for future generations by considering the sustainability of resources and developments that will enhance the prospects and opportunities available for them. They have a collective purpose that drive and even in some cases drag the country to where they want it to be. When leaders learn that their leadership is not about their personal enrichment or destiny but that of the nation and the generations to come, a greater purpose can be born. The essence of good leadership is innovation; leaders have to come up with solutions not politics. One of the celebrated countries in Africa that is purpose-driven would be Rwanda[46]. In spite of having its critics the nation of

Rwanda has been transformed and the lives of its citizens are not what they used to be. Rwanda is not yet there, but it is definitely giving it a good try with a lot of success. It is a fact that for a country to be purpose-driven it needs purpose-driven leadership. It is also a fact that we might not have that many innovative purpose-driven leaders in Africa. To phrase it in another way, it seems the innovative purpose-driven leaders are not taking up their place in Africa.

Several countries in the world have been transformed by leaders who are purpose-driven and every transformed country or continent always has a person or a group of people who are willing to pay the price and position the country for the purpose. A purpose greater than themselves; a purpose that will benefit future generations. Two famous examples in the world are Singapore and the United Arab Emirates. UAE was transformed from a small fishing village to a global real estate hub[47] and Singapore was transformed from a small town to a global financial hub[48]. The common factor in both cases are leadership, innovation and purpose. Even in the bible, it is stated that, "people without purpose or vision cast off restraints or perish"[49].

---

[46]Timothy, C. (2005). Morgan."Purpose Driven in Rwanda.". Christianity Today, 32-36.
[47]Gallup, Inc. (2018, March 14). *The United Arab Emirates at 40: A Success Story*. Gallup.Com. https://news.gallup.com/poll/157061/united-arab-emirates-success-story.aspx
[48]Alam, N. (2015, March 23). *How Lee Kuan Yew transformed Singapore from small town into global financial hub*. The Conversation. https://theconversation.com/how-lee-kuan-yew-transformed-singapore-from-small-town-into-global-financial-hub-39192
[49]Proverbs 29:18 KJV and ESV

On June 5th 1959, Lee Kuan Yew became the first prime minister of a pre-independent Singapore and retained the position for twenty-six years. That is several years less than the alive presidents we have in some African countries. His leadership and foresightedness made him the founding father of one of Asia's smallest but most developed economies. In 1965 when Singapore got independence, that is 5 years after Nigeria (Africa's biggest economy), Lee Kuan Yew took several actions to show his ambition. Singapore joined the United Nations in September 1965. He ensured that government officials were paid well in order to limit corruption. He also developed the Stop at Two Family Planning Campaign which limits families to two kids. Lee Kuan Yew understood the influence of an overgrown population and its threat on economic success. The fact is there is nothing as crippling as a large, young, but underproductive and undereducated population that only consumes[50].

Economic growth was invigorated by what some Singaporeans refer to as, "the big stick and the big carrot." The "carrot" was evident in the development of the country. The "stick" for example is evident when entering the country. On each airport entry card, it is specified in bold letters that the consequence for drug trafficking is "DEATH." Even though Lee was criticized by many for leading the country in a strict autocratic style that muffled political opposition and freedom of the press, his diligent grasp of power and maintenance of stability created the environment for corruption free

---

[50]Filmer, D., & Fox, L. (2014). Youth employment in sub-Saharan Africa. The World Bank.

financial development. The comprehensive financial and economic policy coupled with a corruption free environment and technological development meant many multinational companies chose Singapore as their regional headquarters. It is a fact that some of his approaches would be frowned upon by democratic societies, such as assortative mating where the Social Development Unit would try to ensure that college educated men only marry college educated women.

Lee established the Housing Development Board and the Economic Development Board to cater for housing and employment of Singaporeans. The housing board transformed the space inhibited island into a world-class city that facilitated its citizens to move out of small ghettos into well-planned modern townships, and provided high living conditions for its citizens. Meanwhile, the Development Board gradually built-up Singaporean industries and businesses to create job opportunities for both locals and expatriates to flourish in an economy that could hold up a population rapidly moving out of poverty. Singaporeans had the a*kiasu* mindset. *Kiasu* is a term that implies having a grasping attitude resulting from a fear of missing out on something. Singapore's quest to get ahead made them overachievers and the statistics speak for themselves (as of 2018)[51]:
- Singapore's unemployment was about 2%.

---

[51]Onikute. (2018, March 15). *What Nigeria should learn from Lee Kuan Yew — Singapore's legendary prime minister.* Medium.
https://medium.com/abinibi/what-nigeria-should-learn-from-lee-kuan-yew-singapores-legendary-prime-minister-69ed8bcdf2b8

- It was stated as one of the top countries in which to do business, and has the 6th highest purchasing power in the world.
- The country ranked third in the global education league.
- It is arguably the world's healthiest country.
- About 90% of Singaporeans own their own government-built homes.
- It has one of the lowest crime levels in the world.
- It also stands out as one of the least corrupt nations on the globe.

Lee Kuan Yew, was the recipient of numerous tributes for his remarkable leadership efforts. The long list includes the Nobel Peace Prize; The Woodrow Wilson Award for Public Service; The Russian Order of Friendship Award; and numerous state decorations such as, the Order of Companions of Honor; Order of St. Michael and St. George; and the Order of the Rising Sun, among many others. Lee Kuan Yew was a man with a purpose to transform a small seaside town into a financial giant of global repute. The size of the country's GDP per capita compared to its tiny size and lack of resources is a testament to Lee's success at doing so. His great leadership is evident in all the social advancements that have happened in just the last 45 years or so[52].

By the late 1960s, it was a fact that Asia was one of the poorest continents in the world when it came to income levels, and other indicators with the marginal

---

[52]Kwang, H. F., Ibrahim, Z., Hoong, C. M., Lim, L., Low, I., Lin, R., & Chan, R. (2011). Lee Kuan Yew: hard truths to keep Singapore going. The straits times, 18.

exception of its large population[53]. Within fifty years, Asia has undergone a profound transformation in terms of the economic transformation of its nations and the living conditions of its people. Though the transformation was uneven across countries and amongst people on the continent, this speaks to the fact that anything is possible as long as people and leaders' purpose to make a difference. It is reasonable to propose that by 2050, Asia will be home to more than half of the people on earth and account for more than half of the world's income. It will have an economic and political gravitas in the world that would have been hard to imagine 60 years ago. This was a similar promise that Africa held in the 1960s at the peak of the Pan African movement and the enthusiasm to do and live for a greater purpose. We had leaders who were willing by the names of Toussaint Louverture, Jean-Jacques Dessalines, Haile Selassie, Julius Nyerere, Ahmed Sékou Touré, Kwame Nkrumah, King Sobhuza II, Robert Mugabe, Thomas Sankara and Muammar Gaddafi. Now many African leaders are relegated to a life of opulence, begging and superficial visions that never materialize due to poor leadership[54].

When all is said and done, what happens in government is a result of what happened and is happening in families[55].

---

[53]Nayyar, D. (2019, October 17). *How Asia transformed from the poorest continent in the world into a global economic powerhouse.* The Conversation. https://theconversation.com/how-asia-transformed-from-the-poorest-continent-in-the-world-into-a-global-economic-powerhouse-123729
[54]Adeyemi, S. (2017, May 4). *Africa doesn't need charity, it needs good leadership.* World Economic Forum. https://www.weforum.org/agenda/2017/05/africa-doesn-t-need-charity-it-needs-good-leadership/

Corruption, lack of vision, purpose, lack of ambition, self-centeredness, etc., all originate from how people are brought up in their families. Two things stand out in the case of tiny Singapore and most African countries: corruption and overpopulation. Overpopulation and corruption are both issues that arise and can be resolved at the family level. Overpopulation is not necessarily a real problem on its own[56], it is the lack of sustainable development, limited skills and low productivity in the large population. Of course, government policies can definitely make it work better. When people purpose to make a difference in the life of their nation and their continent, they will commit to the resolve to do their part. If everybody does their part; parents, teachers, politicians and everyone in society for that one greater purpose of becoming a continent of substance, Africa will surely change. Some will argue that if one lives on less than a dollar a day, how can they think of a long-term greater purpose. The fact is it is all a matter of mindsets. It is possible: it has been done before and it can be done again on a continental scale.

As a closing remark, let me share with you the story of an African success that was aborted at its infancy. Thomas Isidore Noël Sankara was a Burkinabé military captain, Marxist revolutionary, pan-Africanist theorist, and President of Burkina Faso from 1983 to 1987. He changed the former French colony of Upper Volta into

---

[55]Onikute. (2018, March 15). *What Nigeria should learn from Lee Kuan Yew — Singapore's legendary prime minister*. Medium.
https://medium.com/abinibi/what-nigeria-should-learn-from-lee-kuan-yew-singapores-legendary-prime-minister-69ed8bcdf2b8
[56]Ellis, E. C. (2013). Overpopulation is not the problem. New York Times, 13, A19.

Burkina Faso, which means, "Land of the Upright Men". Dubbed the "African Che Guevara," during his four-year rule, a nation-wide literacy campaign increased literacy rates from 13% in 1983 to 73% in 1987; some 2.5 million children were vaccinated against meningitis, yellow fever and measles in a matter of weeks; and thousands of health centers opened. Housing, road and railway building projects got under way and 10 million trees were planted[57]. Sankara declared war on corruption and embraced austerity measures though leading by example. As an African head of state, he earned a salary of $450 a month, cutting the salaries of his top government officials and banning the use of expensive cars and first-class airline tickets by his ministers and senior civil servants. He rode a bicycle to work for a while before he upgraded, at his Cabinet's persistence, to one of the cheapest cars available in Burkina Faso at the time, a Renault 5. Under Sankara, the government also prioritized gender equality, working towards the end of female genital mutilation, forced marriages and polygamy[58].

Sankara despised official ceremonies and barred any cult of his personality. It was common to see him walking casually on the streets, jogging or noticeably slipping into the crowd at a public event. He was a motivational orator who spoke with frankness, lucidity and did not waver to

---

[57]Jaffré, B. (2020, April 10). *Facts about Thomas Sankara in Burkina Faso*. My Blog. http://www.thomassankara.net/facts-about-thomas-sankara-in-burkina-faso/?lang=en

[58]Smith, D. (2015, March 6). *Burkina Faso's revolutionary hero Thomas Sankara to be exhumed*. The Guardian. https://www.theguardian.com/world/2015/mar/06/burkina-fasos-revolutionary-hero-thomas-sankara-to-be-exhumed

admit his mistakes publicly. He also expressed moral conviction and objections to heads of powerful nations, and he famously communicated his disapproval of the former French president, François Mitterrand, for hosting the leader of Apartheid South Africa in a state dinner. Sankara was more than a visionary national leader: he loved his people and the continent of Africa; and he was moral and had a strong sense of justice. He used international conferences as podiums to demand leaders to stand up against the deep structural injustices faced by African countries. Sankara condemned the debt owed to the World Bank and International Monetary Fund, which according to him were inherited from colonialism. In the end, Sankara was assassinated by the stereotypical African leaders. On 15th October 1987, Sankara was killed in a coup d'état organized by his colleague, Blaise Compaoré[59]. Compaoré promptly set about "rectifying" Sankara's revolution by installing old and corrupt systems and people. Interestingly, on 8th October 1987, a week before his death, Sankara remarked: *"I have told myself, either I'll finish up an old man somewhere in a library reading books, or I'll meet with a violent end, since we have so many enemies. Once you have accepted that reality, it's just a question of time. It will happen today or tomorrow."* Upon his death, it was believed that his possessions were limited to a car, four bikes, three guitars, a fridge and a broken freezer[60].

---

[59]Neufeld, J. (2019, March 1). *Thomas Sankara Tried to Liberate His Country from the West. Then He Was Murdered*. The Walrus. https://thewalrus.ca/thomas-sankara-tried-to-liberate-his-country-from-the-west-then-he-was-murdered/
[60]Smith, D. (2015, March 6). *Burkina Faso's revolutionary hero Thomas Sankara to be exhumed*. The Guardian.

In Africa over the years, we have had leaders, presidents, prime ministers and politicians in every shape and size. Some did okay and others simply did not care. The fact remains that African's greatest problem is a leadership problem. Thomas Isidore Noël Sankara is an example of what it means to have a leader who cares for the people he leads; a leader who has a vision and a purpose to change the destiny of his nation. Sadly, it was aborted by Africa's biggest nemesis; corrupt leadership[61]. Africa needs leaders with integrity.

---

https://www.theguardian.com/world/2015/mar/06/burkina-fasos-revolutionary-hero-thomas-sankara-to-be-exhumed
[61]Mann, I. (2010). Corrupt and greedy leaders keep Africa poor. Business Times Sunday Times, 2.

Respect

"When you are content to be simply yourself and don't compare or compete, everyone will respect you."
Lao Tzu

"Respect for ourselves guides our morals; respect for others guides our manners."
Laurence Sterne

"We must have respect for both plumbers and our philosophers, or neither our pipes or our theories will hold water."
John. W. Garner

The fact is that respect never runs out of style and in truth it is the hallmark of a cultured person and the bedrock of a civilized society. The author, Sesanti[62] argued that historically, in African culture, respect was not only reserved for the elders but it was also rendered to the physically weak and vulnerable. He claimed that traditional *African* societies endorsed reciprocity between adults and children and the rest of those who shared the same space. African culture is about respect, but when you look much closer under the surface you might see something different. This respect might be superficial because the type of respect that is shown when a person is present and not shown when the person is absent is questionable. One of the most critical elements that keep societies robust is respect. Respect of life, respect of freedom and respect of property.

The **term respect** originates from the Latin word, "*respectus*" which means attention, regard or consideration. It can be defined as "esteem for, or a sense of worth or excellence of a person, a quality, or something considered as a manifestation of a personal quality or ability".[63] In our world, respect is an overall assessment you give someone based on many factors such as what that person is doing with their life, how they treat you and others, whether they are honest or not and if they seem to consistently do good things, large or small, for other people. It is a concept that refers to the ability to value and honour another person, both his or her words

---

[62]Sesanti, S. (2010). The concept of 'respect 'in African culture in the context of journalism practice: An Afrocentric intervention. *Communicatio: South African Journal for Communication Theory and Research, 36*(3), 343-358.
[63]Salazar, A. (2019, October 2). *Respect: What is it, types, examples, learn and teach respect*. Health, Brain and Neuroscience. https://blog.cognifit.com/respect/

and actions, even though we do not approve or share everything he or she does. It is accepting the other person and not trying to change them.

One of the biggest indicators that Africans might not be as respectful is the fact that many Africans don't respect time and more so, other people's time[64]. Coming late might seem like an insignificant thing but it does communicate respect for self and others. As Africans, it appears we don't respect our environment and the property of others. Just move around in most African cities, with the exception of the posh neighbourhoods, dirt and litter are everywhere[65]. It is not uncommon to find someone in a very expensive car throwing their empty bottle of water out the window. Strangely, these very same Africans will not do that when they are in Europe or North America. That simply communicates the fact that they have no respect for their continent, country and countrymen. It is not uncommon in Africa to see the wealthy and the powerful treat the less fortunate like trash. This is accentuated by land grabbing, abuse of power and exploitation of the poor[66]. It is not uncommon to hear people ask, "do you know who I am?" as a means to flex their power and influence and to dehumanize their fellow African. A lot of Africans don't have respect[67].

---

[64] Osawe, C. O. (2017). Time management: an imperative factor to effective service delivery in the Nigeria public service. International Journal of Development and Management Review, 12(1), 152-167.

[65] Southall, R. (2018, May 9). Littering in South Africa is the expression of wider selfish – and costly – culture. The Conversation. https://theconversation.com/littering-in-south-africa-is-the-expression-of-wider-selfish-and-costly-culture-96186

[66] Justesen, M. K., & Bjørnskov, C. (2014). Exploiting the poor: Bureaucratic corruption and poverty in Africa. World Development, 58, 106-115.

[67] Modern Ghana. (2013, April 26). THE NEGATIVE ASPECT OF RESPECT IN

We can superficially show it but it's just at face value due to cultural obligation. We respect the rich and powerful and sometimes the elderly but we don't have respect for our fellow humans when we perceive they are poor and powerless. They are treated as less human. We might fear but we don't respect. Of course, that is my view and I can't say it is the case for all Africans.

Interestingly, in some families, being disrespectful is a sign that they are truly wealthy and powerful. Their children are raised to bulldoze those they feel are inferior and to only give regard to those who are perceived to be their equal or superior. The fact however is that everything human, by virtue of being born a human being needs and deserves to be respected. It is part of according human dignity to human beings. Sadly, nowadays we even have Africans who put more value on animals over human life[68]. That is pure evil.

Every now and then, I get a student with such mentality, especially one of my undergraduate classes. As the years pass, it is not uncommon to find some students come into class with their earphones plugged in their ears; giving presentations while chewing gum; and even in some cases, answering phone calls in the class. That has led to the need to include respect in my class orientation. In my respect talk, I firstly remind students that they have to respect themselves. Respecting themselves means they

---

AFRICAN CULTURE. https://www.modernghana.com/news/460727/the-negative-aspect-of-respect-in-african-culture.html

[68] Bry, D. (2016, June 2). I can't believe I have to say it: a human life is worth more than a gorilla's. The Guardian. https://www.theguardian.com/commentisfree/2016/may/31/human-life-more-gorilla-killed-cincinnati-boy-fell-enclosure

have to behave in a manner that is worthy of being respected. Secondly, I tell them the need to respect others in terms of how they behave around others and how they treat others. Thirdly, I tell them they have to respect property: the university property, theirs and other people's property. I always conclude the talk with the fact that I will be held to the same standard that I demand of them: I will treat every student with respect as long as they show that they deserve it. The approach has been a success. Most of my students, present and former claim they know me to be a principled and respectful person, and I have had the privilege of being honoured by them in the presence of my children: from being bumped up to the VIP section in the cinema because the manager was my former student to my children being given preferential treatment on their travels because someone came across their surname and discovered they are related to me. I am personally not one to ask for preferential treatment, but a person who shows respect to others will always be respected by others. It is simply the law of reciprocity.

At this point, it is important to note that respect is not the same as fear. Respect germinates from admiration and reverence. Fear is the consequence of the possible wrath that an individual can dish out because of their power and position. This fear has created the cult of personality in Africa and it has been assumed to be respect. A cult of personality[69] is a result of when a political leader (e.g., president) or individuals of power and influence, in general, use the techniques of mass media

---

[69] Mudde, C., & Kaltwasser, C. R. (2017). *Populism: A very short introduction*. Oxford University Press.

and propaganda to manipulate the public. They create a flawless, gallant, and reverential image of the leader or said person, often through outrageous flattery and praise. In some cases, these leaders can even link their legitimacy to the divine (apotheosis), ultimately the overarching element is fear. To object might be costly to those who oppose the individual and might lead to grave consequences. It is often seen in totalitarian or authoritarian countries, some of which we have in Africa under the guise of democracy[70]. In such countries, the rule of law is absent and the rule of man is the order of the day. The rule of man is characterized by a society in which one person, regime, or a group of persons, rules arbitrarily. This individual leader or regime exercises complete authority and is not limited by any law. He as a person exists outside the law. This means this individual or regime can do whatever they want with no respect for the law because they are the law.

The lack of respect for the rule of law is the lack of respect for human life and society. This can be very dangerous and it is a breeding ground for corruption and extrajudicial killings. A leader who does not respect the law of the land, should not be respected and should not even lead in the first place. Some will argue that there are two types of respect; respect for a person as a human being and respect for a person as an authority[71]. I will

---

[70]Diamond, L. (2008). Progress and retreat in Africa: The rule of law versus the big man. *Journal of Democracy, 19*(2), 138-149.

[71]Stackelberg, H. (2018, March 31). *Respect and Power: there are two types of each, don't confuse them.* Medium. https://medium.com/mugging-the-muse/respect-and-power-there-are-two-types-of-each-dont-confuse-them-1aa174a1dabf

argue that at the end of it all, respect is about the influence which can result in power (or authority) but should be accorded to all human beings, regardless of age, race, gender or creed. Respect out of fear tends to end up badly for the "respected". Africa needs people who value and respect others for who they are and the contribution they can make. Everyone has potential as long as they are given the opportunity and the chance to unlock it. Respect costs nothing but it yields great returns.

Trustworthiness

"Never trust someone that claims they care nothing of what society thinks of them. Instead of conquering obstacles, they simply pretend they don't exist."
Tiffany Madison

"In leadership, life and all things, it's far wiser to judge people by their deeds than their speech - their track record rather than their talk."
Rasheed Ogunlaru

"Whoever is careless with the truth in small matters cannot be trusted with important matters."
Albert Einstein

Trust is very important to humans and as humans, everything we do is influenced by trust. Honesty is the foundation of trust and trustworthiness. The moral obligation to be honest necessitates us to speak and to act only in ways that stimulate and validate trust. Trust has to be earned. It is very common for people not to trust others these days. They will tell you the world is a different place now and to trust just anybody is to be naïve.

However, trust is essential and it influences everything. Being trusted by others is one of the things you must achieve to go far in life and to realize success as a person, family, society or country. Honesty and trust are an important part of bonding, for they are a necessity in any personal relationship. An individual who is not trustworthy is usually perceived to be worthless, and would probably not have true friends. On the other hand, an individual who is trustworthy is often perceived to be highly valuable and reliable, and will characteristically be fiercely backed up and protected by others around him or her. As stated, earlier, trust is a core and significant building block in human relationships, and one can easily see how a lack of trust can lead to the complete destruction of any and all relationships. A marriage without trust cannot function; a society that lacks trust cannot thrive; and a country deficient in trust will not last.

Trust is a two-way thing; you can only be trusted if you are trustworthy. There is a high chance that the person you don't trust probably doesn't trust you either. This is because even if one party is trustworthy, the untrustworthiness of the other party will damage the relationship. It is almost like saying, "to a hammer, every problem is a nail" and to a dishonest person, nobody is trustworthy. In the words of Henry Stimson, the American politician and Lawyer: "The only way to make a man trustworthy is to trust him." I would advise caution along with the benefit of doubt. The easiest way a person can prove their trustworthiness is by keeping their word. An individual's word acts as a sort of promise that one will or will not do something, and one must always keep these promises in order to build trust with others. As humans, we are designed to be in relationships with others. This has formed the basis of families, societies and nations. Being able to trust each other means that we can do more together and this can be reflected in countries and societies.

During the early stages of the Covid-19 pandemic, through the media, I was able to deduct that some countries and parts of society lack trust in the leadership of their countries, and these societies reflected that lack of trust by the fact that they believed the whole thing was a hoax. In some African countries, for example, many believed that the pandemic was used as a means for government officials to fill up their pockets. They believed the lockdown was not called for and that only the powerful and influential were benefiting from the entire situation. This lack of trust provided the hotbed for fake news to thrive[72].

---

[72]Reality Check Team. (2020, April 24). *No, hot steam is not a cure for coronavirus.* BBC News. https://www.bbc.com/news/world-africa-51710617

The serious lack of trust in Africa is proven by research findings and its repercussions on everyday life. Approximately 70% of Africans believe political party leaders are purely self-interest seekers and are to no extent interested in representing the people's interests. In a survey across 36 African countries, less than half of the respondent said they trusted their MPs (48%) and local councillors (46%)[73]. Similarly, according to the 2015 Global Corruption Report by Transparency International (TI)[74], the police is professed to be the most corrupt institution in the African continent. 20 African countries stood out of the 36 countries worldwide where the police was perceived as the most corrupt institution. According to the study, 31% of the people who came into contact with the police reported having paid a bribe. The bribery prevalence rate of the police was 75% or more in seven countries, including six African countries. The report further states that the judiciary followed behind the police in the most corrupt institutions. This is just part of the picture. There is more when you speak to the average African; there is a lack of trust for almost every single section: medical[75], educational[76], media[77], religious

---

[73]Aiko, R., Akinocho, H., & Lekorwe, M. (2016). Job performance of MPs, local councillors: Are representatives serving voters or themselves?.
[74]Wambua, P. M. (2015, November 2). *Police Corruption in Africa Undermines Trust, but Support for Law Enforcement Remains Strong*. Africa Portal. https://www.africaportal.org/publications/police-corruption-in-africa-undermines-trust-but-support-for-law-enforcement-remains-strong/
[75]Hsiao, A., Vogt, V., & Quentin, W. (2019). Effect of corruption on perceived difficulties in healthcare access in sub-Saharan Africa. *PloS one, 14*(8), e0220583.
[76]AFP. (2020, March 5). *"Sex-for-marks" don sacked by university*. New Vision. https://www.newvision.co.ug/news/1480228/sex-marks-sacked-university
[77]Al Jazeera. (2015, December 27). *Bribes and brown envelopes: Nigeria's "journalists."* Nigeria | Al Jazeera. https://www.aljazeera.com/programmes/listeningpost/2015/12/bribes-brown-

institutions[78], etc.

The high level of distrust that exists in Africa, probably like other parts of the world, shows that these institutions are not dependable, reliable or even credible enough to fulfill their mandate. A simple solution to this problem is that those who are trust worthy should be voted into office, and if there is none, then trustworthy people who want to see change should run for office and be voted in by others. It is of course easier said than done. The dynamics are not that simple. The simple fact is that people end up with the types of leaders they deserve and thus the institutions that come with it. When people choose to be silent and allow what is wrong to thrive, they are as guilty as those doing it.Edmund Burke, the Irish philosopher and politician, said it best: "The only thing necessary for the triumph of evil is for good men to do nothing." The lack of trust, dishonesty and corruption has thrived because the good men and women of the continent chose to do nothing and the distrust continues to grow.

We need to build trust in Africa, among Africans and out of Africa. We need to become people who are credible and dependable. We need trust to become a core African value in actions, not just words. It does not matter how many schools, hospitals, roads and other infrastructure are built as long as there is a lack of trust, they are all

---

envelopes-nigeria-journalists-151227175941010.html
[78]Mfumbusa, B. (2010, August 11). *The Church is Growing. Corruption is Growing*. Religion Unplugged.
https://religionunplugged.com/news/index.php/2010/08/11/the-church-is-growing-corruption-is-growing

bound to fail. If we can't trust the teachers in the schools, the doctors in the hospitals, the drivers on the roads and the builders of the nation, then we are all standing on a giant sinkhole. It is therefore important that we all take up the responsibility of being trustworthy as individuals in our respective sphere of influence.

The beauty about being trustworthy is that you don't have to tell people; they will see it for themselves in your words and your conduct. Several ways have been suggested on becoming trustworthy, but when all is said and done, trust begins with self. As Stephen Covey puts it: "The process of building trust is an interesting one, but it begins with yourself, with what I call self-trust, and with your own credibility, your own trustworthiness. If you think about it, it's hard to establish trust with others if you can't trust yourself."[79] If you don't trust yourself with money, people, power, time and resources in general, who can trust you with theirs? To become trustworthy, one has to[80]:

- **Be authentic** – Be yourself and stay true to your values and morals. Stand for what you believe in and don't be swayed by fads or popular trends. Live by your convictions. At least people will respect you for being sincere.
- **Be transparent and accountable** – Let people know who you are and what you stand for so they can hold you to the standards you profess. If you

---

[79]Covey, S. R., & Merrill, R. R. (2006). *The speed of trust: The one thing that changes everything*. Simon and schuster.
[80]Wachter, H. (2018, November 15). *7 Ways to Become Trustworthy*. Experience Life. https://experiencelife.com/article/7-ways-to-become-trustworthy/

lack morals, they will know to avoid you and if you have values, they will see if you truly reflect them in your conduct.
- **Keep promises** – When you make promises, make sure you keep them and if you know you cannot keep the promise, don't make it. In cases where you feel it is out of your control; take a step to give an alternative or boldly go and face the music.
- **Keep confidences** – Be a person people can confide in and rest assured that their secret is safe with you. The more people's confidence you keep, the more trustworthy you become and word travels. Definitely, avoid gossiping and gossips.
- **Set and respect boundaries** – As mentioned in the earlier chapter, respect yourself and respect others. Know what your limits are and what is and is not appropriate. This will also reflect your values.
- **Be vulnerable** – Show people that you are approachable and you can relate to them and their situation. This gives people the confidence that you have similar values and interests as them.
- **Have discussions in person** – Meet and interact with people in person because face-to-face communication is the richest communication channel in the world. People are able to see you and read you. They can see your nonverbal communication and deduce traits such as sincerity, kindness, and warmth. All this cannot be done in writing or even on the phone at times. Don't send someone else if you can do it yourself to show your respect for the person.

- **Serve others** – Be selfless to others and understanding to them as you can be. Show care and compassion. Be willing to go the extra mile for others for nothing in return.
- **Own your mistakes** – When you fail, be the first to accept and try to make restitution for the mistake if someone has been hurt. It takes a real mature person to acknowledge their mistakes, and an even better one to be willing to do something about it.
- **Show your gratitude** – Always look for the good in things and look for the silver lining in every situation.

Trust is very important. Again, in the words of Stephen Covey: "The first job of a leader—at work or at home—is to inspire trust. It is to bring out the best in people by entrusting them with meaningful stewardships, and to create an environment in which high-trust interaction inspires creativity and possibility." Just imagine an Africa with leaders who operate with such levels of trust. These are the types of leaders people are willing to stake their lives on; leaders who have both your back and interest at heart. Leaders who you are willing to follow and support even if you don't completely understand their vision because you know they are trustworthy. We all must inspire trust to have an impact on our societies, countries and even our generation.

Fairness

"Equality is not a concept. It's not something we should be striving for. It's a necessity. Equality is like gravity. We need it to stand on this earth as men and women, and the misogyny that is in every culture is not a true part of the human condition. It is life out of balance, and that imbalance is sucking something out of the soul of every man and woman who's confronted with it. We need equality."
Joss Whedon

"Your level of integrity, ethical behaviour and sense of fairness will contribute to your success – or lack of it – over the long term."
Ross Wilson

> "Live so that when your children think of fairness and integrity, they think of you."
>
> **H. Jackson Brown Jr.**

To be fair, you have to have integrity. It is a fact that most humans, if not all, want to be treated fairly. Sadly, not everyone behaves in a fair manner to their fellow humans. Fairness is the concept of treating people equally without any discrimination or favouritism. Justice is often about superseding principles and fairness is usually about how those principles are applied to a specific set of circumstances or a particular situation. In theory, a just society is a fair society. Fairness and equality are vital ingredients for a successful society. Fairness, however, is not the same thing as equality and we need both if we are going to be not only a decent society but a successful country. The absence of equality might imply the absence of fairness and thus injustice.

According to Wikipedia, "justice is a concept of moral rightness based ethics, rationality, law, natural law, religion, equity and fairness, as well as the administration of the law, taking into account the inalienable and inborn rights of all human beings and citizens, the right of all people and individuals to equal protection before the law of their civil rights, without discrimination on the basis of race, gender, sexual orientation, gender identity, national origin, color, ethnicity, religion, disability, age, wealth, or other characteristics, and is further regarded as being inclusive of social justice"[81]. Though my focus in this chapter is not on justice, we cannot talk about fairness without justice and equality. *Equality* is about ensuring that every individual has an equal opportunity to make the most of their lives and talents, while fairness or equity is defined as just or appropriate behaviour in a given the circumstance; it is the quality of being impartial. On the basis of justice, all humans should be treated fairly (or equitably) and equally. This is tricky because on paper everybody agrees, but in practice and in truth, many people don't believe all humans are equal. This belief that all humans are not equal has led to challenges in fairness (or equity). The absence of fairness, equality, and justice will always lead to chaos and division in any society.

One of the most common observations on the African continent and the world for that matter is that some people are above the law. It is common knowledge that when a wealthy or famous person breaks the law, the consequences are not as grave as they would be for the average citizen. This is very much the practice in Africa where billions are embezzled and misappropriated and the culprits walk free. In some cases, they even become heroes to those who benefited from the crime. While you'll find the "small fish" or political rivals are being arrested, taken to court, and imprisoned for years[82]. This pattern repeats itself in every aspect of the African society: from how you are treated in a hospital to how

---

[81]Wikipedia contributors. (2020, July 14). *Justice*. Wikipedia. https://en.wikipedia.org/wiki/Justice

[82]Mills, L. C. (2017). Catching the 'big fish': The (ab) use of corruption-related prosecutions across sub-Saharan Africa. *Development Policy Review, 35*, O160-O177.

you are treated in a restaurant; in spite of the fact that you are paying for the service in some cases.

African societies are crippled by the vices that undermine equality, fairness and definitely justice. These vices account for the uneven distribution of wealth, health and education among others in several African countries. These vices are what evoke the sentiment that several African countries whisper the need to break up, regardless of the high cost of secession[83]. From Algeria to Zimbabwe, Africa reeks with tribalism, nepotism, religious segregation and all-ostracism[84]. In spite of the fact that the Black Lives Matter movement was in full swing and is warranted, I felt a lot of Africans (not African Americans) do not have the right to claim to be discriminated against since hatred towards their fellow Africans is endemic. Africans are as guilty as the others who marginalize and oppress, but even worse, Africans do the same to their fellow Africans. It has always been a historic problem in Africa, from the transatlantic slave trade[85] to contemporary Africa; to say it simply, some Africans hate fellow Africans. Please note that I am not saying all Africans, in fact it might even be a minority (a fraction), but this minority causes a lot of damage to what can and should be. It is a crab in a bucket mentality[86].

---

[83]Ekeke, A. C., & Lubisi, N. (2019). Secession in Africa: an African Union Dilemma. *African Security Review, 28*(3-4), 245-260.
[84]Human Rights Watch. (2020, July 17). *South Africa: Attacks on Foreign Nationals*. https://www.hrw.org/news/2019/04/15/south-africa-attacks-foreign-nationals
[85]Campbell, J. (2019, September 26). *Confronting Africa's Role in the Slave Trade*. Council on Foreign Relations. https://www.cfr.org/blog/confronting-africas-role-slave-trade
[86] Simmons, A. (2014). The crab syndrome. Antuan Simmons.

The ones down don't want you to climb up and the ones up don't want you to come up either[87]. Some Africans feel better seeing their fellow Africans miserable, both home and away, and in some cases, they are even willing to compromise the peace and security of their country[88].

It is a fact that with some early exemptions, Europeans slave traders were not able to independently enter the West and Central African interior to enslave Africans and force them onto ships bound for the Americas. They did not have the know-how, the force and the strong enough constitution (the guts). Instead, European traders largely depended on a network of African monarchs and traders to capture and bring enslaved Africans from numerous coastal and interior regions to slave fortresses on the West and Central African coasts. Several of these monarchs and traders acquired captives as a result of military and political conflict, but several also engaged in slave trading purely for profit. It is argued that up to 90% of Africans abducted from the continent during the transatlantic slave trade were traded or sold to the Europeans by fellow Africans[89].

In modern-day Africa, it is not uncommon in many African societies to find that families don't want their

---

[87] GhanaWeb. (2016, February 11). Crab Mentality: "The case of Africa." Ghana Web. https://www.ghanaweb.com/GhanaHomePage/features/Crab-Mentality-The-case-of-Africa-414734

[88] Sule, A. O. (2019, August 12). Racism harms black people most. It's time to recognise "anti-blackness." The Guardian.
https://www.theguardian.com/commentisfree/2019/aug/09/black-people-racism-anti-blackness-discrimination-minorities

[89] Gates, H. L. (2010). Ending the slavery blame-game. *New York Times*, 22.

children to marry into another tribe or religion but strangely they might be willing to allow their children to marry a European or American. What does this mindset say about the society, the family? This mindset exists among educated and well-travelled people who are willing to defend their views with the argument of "our culture". But what they are truly saying is, "we are not equals." It is not uncommon to find that in some African countries the government is made of up of mostly a single tribe, regardless of the fact that the country has a diversity of tribes and cultures, and in some cases, a single family and their cronies run the country[90]. It is a pattern that a lot of Africans vote along the lines of tribes and religion and give very little regard to political substance or ideals[91]. They simply don't care; they just want "our people" to be in power. What they truly mean is that we are better than others and we don't trust "others" to run the country. These mindsets have a very strong hold on the African continent and remain one of the biggest burdens faced by the younger generation who are not interested in differences, but in common grounds. They just want to change their situation; marry who they want to marry; and vote for who they believe truly speaks to their ideals for the future. All humans, regardless of race, tribe or creed, should be judged by the content of their character. Not prejudged!

It all comes back to fairness, equality and justice. The

---

[90]Savage, J. (2019, August 14). *Ethics of Nepotism Deeply Rooted in African Governments.* Modern Ghana. https://www.modernghana.com/news/950067/ethics-of-nepotism-deeply-rooted-in-african-govern.html
[91]Juma, C. (2012, November 27). *Viewpoint: How tribalism stunts African democracy.* BBC News. https://www.bbc.com/news/world-africa-20465752

belief that in spite of the fact that we have different backgrounds, religions and histories; we are equals. This means I will treat my fellow countryman or woman with respect by being fair. To borrow from the American declaration of independence, indeed: "...all men are created equal, that they are endowed by their Creator with certain unalienable Rights, that among these are Life, Liberty and the pursuit of Happiness."[92] It is a profound claim that carries little power when it is not truly planted in the hearts of people. Truly successful societies are founded on the idea of fairness and equality. Everyone, regardless of gender, race, age, religious beliefs or any other personal characteristic should have the right to equal and fair treatment. A prosperous society or country is where every citizen has the rights, freedom and access to national resources like any other citizen to excel in life and to find fulfillment. I personally believe that it is a moral obligation to help others if you have the ability, in their pursuit of purpose, fulfillment and happiness.

Societies that are truly fair and equal are more likely to deal with and try to eliminate discrimination and to provide equal opportunities which can enable individuals and families to positively impact society and the economy. Innovation, talent, leadership and others are not limited or restricted to a group of people. Every human in a fair society should have the freedom to explore their potential within the confines of the law without impeding on others' freedom. Several studies[93]

---

[92] Congress, U. S. (1776). Declaration of independence. *Available in: http://memory. loc. gov/cgi-bin/ampage*.
[93] Paulus, M., & Moore, C. (2017). Preschoolers' generosity increases with

have shown that fairness and thinking about others (as equals) leads to a higher personal well-being and increased sense of purpose.

The major benefit of fairness, equality and justice in a country is unity and it is a fact that when people come together and put their minds and heart into something, anything is possible. Research confirms that united societies do not have to choose between economic success and greater equality and fairness as perceived by some. United societies harness the benefits across a bundle of health and social outcomes, which includes the fact that people live longer and healthier lives; people are less likely to develop mental health issues; educational outcomes are better; communities are more cohesive; and violent crime is less likely. And these benefits do not just improve the lives of those with the least; they can be seen across all sections of society. And importantly it greatly reduces the cost of public services to remedy and prevent these ills, which in turn leaves more capacity for the economy to grow and increase overall prosperity[94].

In simple terms, be fair to people no matter who they are because, like you, they have hope and aspirations and want a better life. If the institutions in the country reflect fairness and everybody is treated equally, I am sure there will be more patriotism. People will be willing to pay their taxes because they feel it is used for the right things. It brings people together. Even though people's rights are

---

understanding of the affective benefits of sharing. *Developmental science*, 20(3), e12417.

[94] Adigüzel, Y., Flomenbom, O., & Coban, G. U. (2017). From the physiocrats to fairness in nations. Reports in Advances of Physical Sciences, 1(01), 1750001.

their entitlement, it is important that these rights are fairly exercised. In an unfair society where public servants live like kings on tax payers and everything is manipulated to benefit a group of people, there will always be trouble. As the good book states: "Every kingdom divided against itself is brought to desolation, and every city or house divided against itself shall not stand"[95]. We need Africa to stand. We need unity. We need fairness.

---

[95] Matthew 12:25 NKJV

Compassion

"Where there is no human connection, there is no compassion. Without compassion, then community, commitment, loving-kindness, human understanding, and peace all shrivel. Individuals become isolated, the isolated turn cruel, and the tragic hovers in the forms of domestic and civil violence. Art and literature are antidotes to that."
Susan Vreeland

"There is a nobility in compassion, a beauty in empathy, a grace in forgiveness."
John Connolly

"Our human compassion binds us the

one to the other - not in pity or patronizingly, but as human beings who have learnt how to turn our common suffering into hope for the future."

Nelson Mandela

Compassion is very important in life and in society. Some even argue that compassion is the most powerful force in the world. Compassion itself as a word has its origin in the Latin word, *"pati"*, which means to suffer, and the prefix "com" - means with. Thus, the word compassion, originates from *"compati"*, which literally means to "suffer with".[96] This is confirmed by other scholars who pointed out that the etymology of "compassion" is Latin, which means "co-suffering."[97] The meaning of the word itself is found in its origin, but several people have given their definitions of compassion and it varies but has a common thread running through them. Compassion is valued by many world religions, including Islam, Judaism and Christianity[98].

Sadly, it is a proven fact that highly religious people are less motivated by compassion in comparison to nonreligious people[99]; a point Jesus himself made in the

---

[96] Compassion. (2019, September 19). *What Is Compassion? Understanding the Meaning of Compassion*. Compassion. https://www.compassion.com/child-development/meaning-of-compassion/
[97] Lopez, S. J. (Ed.). (2011). *The encyclopedia of positive psychology*. John Wiley & Sons.
[98] van Ments, L., Roelofsma, P., & Treur, J. (2018). Modelling the effect of religion on human empathy based on an adaptive temporal–causal network model. *Computational Social Networks*, 5(1), 1.

story of the good Samaritan (Luke 10:25-37). Some more recent studies dispute this claim.[100] Among emotion researchers, it is defined as the feeling that arises when you are confronted with another's suffering and feel motivated to relieve that suffering.[101] According to Karen Armstrong, a religious historian, the word for compassion in Semitic languages – rahamanut in Hebrew and rahman in Arabic – is etymologically associated with the word for womb, suggesting the mother's love for her child as an archetypal expression of our compassion[102]. According to Aristotle, "compassion is a pain at an impression of destructive or painful evil as befalling one who doesn't deserve it, and which one might expect oneself or someone close to oneself to suffer, when it seems nearby."*[103]*

On the African continent, like other parts of the world, we need more compassion. The lack of compassion is evident in our everyday life and we can personally attest to the fact that there have been cases we did not show compassion to our fellow humans. The absence of compassion is what has led to several vices in our society such as indifference, intolerance and injustice. True

---

[99] Anwar, Y. (2012). Highly Religious People Are Less Motivated by Compassion Than are Non-Believers. *Media Relations*.

[100] Jacobs, T. (2017, June 14). *Religious People Tend to Be More Compassionate*. Pacific Standard. https://psmag.com/social-justice/reason-and-empathy-are-separate-but-compatible

[101] The Greater Good Science Center. (n.d.). *Compassion Definition | What Is Compassion*. Greater Good. Retrieved August 2, 2020, from https://greatergood.berkeley.edu/topic/compassion/definition

[102] Jinpa, T. (2016). *A fearless heart: How the courage to be compassionate can transform our lives*. Avery.

[103] Skills You Need. (n.d.). *Compassion*. Skillsyouneed.Com. Retrieved August 2, 2020, from https://www.skillsyouneed.com/ps/compassion.html

compassion is able to replace judgment with acceptance because it makes no distinction between age, ethnicity, gender or disability. Compassion freely embraces the rich diversity of the human tapestry by treating everyone as equals. It benefits both those who receive it and those who share it. Every person on earth desires it, and every human being deserves it. People like Mother Teresa, Martin Luther King Jr., St. Francis of Assisi, Nelson Mandela, Mahatma Gandhi, and so many others are the embodiment of compassion and how it can change the world. The connection of suffering with another person brings compassion beyond sympathy into the realm of empathy and this has led to amazing changes in human history. It is important to note that compassion is not the same as empathy or altruism in spite of the fact that the concepts are associated. Empathy denotes our ability to take the viewpoint of and feel the emotions of another person; compassion takes it a step further when those feelings and thoughts include the desire to actually help[104]. Altruism, on the other hand, is the caring, self-sacrificing behavior normally provoked by feelings of compassion[105]. It is however possible to feel compassion without acting on it. Similarly, altruism isn't always inspired by compassion; in some cases, moral conviction can be the basis of altruism, among others.

It is a fact that a person cannot give what they don't have,

---

[104] Jazaieri, H., Jinpa, G. T., McGonigal, K., Rosenberg, E. L., Finkelstein, J. Simon-Thomas, E., Cullen, M., Doty, J. R., Gross, J. J., Goldin, P. R. (2012). Enhancing compassion: A randomized controlled trial of a compassion cultivation training program. J Happiness Stud. doi: 10.1007/s10902-012-9373-z
[105] Weng, H. Y., Fox, A. S., Shackman, A. J., Stodola, D. E., Caldwell, J. Z., Olson, M. C., ... & Davidson, R. J. (2013). Compassion training alters altruism and neural responses to suffering. Psychological science, 24(7), 1171-1180.

thus the need to understand self-compassion. Self-compassion is a vital element of compassion that is often over-looked. *Self-compassion* is the ability to turn understanding, acceptance, and love inward. Self-compassion is about being forgiving and empathetic towards yourself because of *the fact that you are human and you have* shortcomings. Self-compassion simply requires you to treat your own mistakes the way you treat the mistakes of others, to treat yourself with objectivity instead of obsessing over your shortcomings.[106] Self-compassion is showing compassion to one's self in situations of apparent inadequacy, failure, or general suffering. Self-compassion is made up of three main components: self-kindness, common humanity, and mindfulness.[107] Perfection is impossible, but we should always aspire to it, but don't berate yourselves over what you can't control. Always do your best and be proud of who you are and your efforts no matter how small or insignificant they may appear. In simple terms, self-compassion is about being less self-critical and self-damning. It is always knowing that you will fail like others and will always need to get up and try again, just like others.

Volumes upon volumes of studies have shown how compassion is beneficial not only to society, but to individuals and even to their personal health.[108] Research

---

[106] Joeng, J. R., & Turner, S. L. (2015). Mediators between self-criticism and depression: Fear of compassion, self-compassion, and importance to others. Journal of Counseling Psychology, 62(3), 453.
[107] Neff, K. (2011). Self-compassion. Hachette UK.
[108] Shapira, L. B., & Mongrain, M. (2010). The benefits of self-compassion and optimism exercises for individuals vulnerable to depression. The Journal of Positive Psychology, 5(5), 377-389.

has confirmed that when we show compassion, our heart rate slows down and we secrete a powerful hormone released when we hug or kiss loved ones that plays a huge role in pair bonding. It is called oxytocin, also known as the "cuddle hormone" or the "love hormone"[109]. Oxytocin also "lights up" parts of our brains associated with empathy, care giving and feelings of pleasure, which often drives our desire to approach and care for other people. The following are confirmed findings on compassion which are based on research:

1. Compassion facilitates social connection among adults and children. Social connection is indispensable to adaptive human functioning due to the fact that it is linked to higher self-esteem, empathy, well-being; and higher interpersonal orientation.[110]
2. Compassion is associated with increased levels of happiness.[111]
3. Compassion is linked to higher levels of overall well-being.[112]
4. Studies show that compassionate love is related to higher patient survival rates, even after regulating substance use effects and social support.[113]

---

[109]Moberg, K. U., & Moberg, K. (2003). The oxytocin factor: Tapping the hormone of calm, love, and healing. Da Capo Press.

[110]Seppala, E., Rossomando, T., & Doty, J. R. (2013). Social connection and compassion: Important predictors of health and well-being. Social Research: An International Quarterly, 80(2), 411-430.

[111]Shapira, L. B., & Mongrain, M. (2010). The benefits of self-compassion and optimism exercises for individuals vulnerable to depression. The Journal of Positive Psychology, 5(5), 377-389.

[112]Zessin, U., Dickhäuser, O., & Garbade, S. (2015). The relationship between self-compassion and well-being: A meta-analysis. Applied Psychology: Health and Well-Being, 7(3), 340-364.

[113]Ironson, G., Kremer, H., & Lucette, A. (2018). Compassionate love predicts

5. Patient-reported clinician empathy and compassion is connected to increased patient satisfaction and lower distress.[114]
6. It has been documented that a doctor's expression of compassion for just a few seconds are connected to reduced patient anxiety.[115]
7. It was observed that the relationship between religion and aggression was weakened among youths rated higher in compassion and self-control.[116]
8. Compassion encourages positive parenting by improving parent-child relationships (i.e., more affection).[117]
9. Compassion within a classroom setting is linked to increased cooperation and better learning.[118]
10. Studies show in education that compassion for teachers as expressed by colleagues is related to higher levels of teacher job satisfaction, organizational commitment, and sense of emotional vigor.[119]

---

long-term survival among people living with HIV followed for up to 17 years. The Journal of Positive Psychology, 13(6), 553-562.

[114] Lelorain, S., Brédart, A., Dolbeault, S., & Sultan, S. (2012). A systematic review of the associations between empathy measures and patient outcomes in cancer care. Psycho-Oncology, 21(12), 1255-1264.

[115] Fogarty, L. A., Curbow, B. A., Wingard, J. R., McDonnell, K., & Somerfield, M. R. (1999). Can 40 seconds of compassion reduce patient anxiety?. Journal of Clinical Oncology, 17(1), 371-371.

[116] Shepperd, J. A., Miller, W. A., & Smith, C. T. (2015). Religiousness and aggression in adolescents: The mediating roles of self-control and compassion. Aggressive behavior, 41(6), 608-621.

[117] Duncan, L. G., Coatsworth, J. D., & Greenberg, M. T. (2009). A model of mindful parenting: Implications for parent–child relationships and prevention research. Clinical child and family psychology review, 12(3), 255-270.

[118] Hart, S., & Hodson, V. K. (2004). The compassionate classroom: Relationship based teaching and learning. PuddleDancer Press.

[119] Eldor, L., & Shoshani, A. (2016). Caring relationships in school staff: Exploring

11. Self-compassion has several proven psychological benefits, such as reduced Post-traumatic stress disorder (PTSD) symptom severity.[120]
12. Self-compassion is linked to more positive aging.[121]
13. Self-compassion is linked to various aspects of general well-being.[122]
14. Self-compassion cushions the negative impact of stress.[123]

From the stated studies, you can see that compassion can truly change lives and societies. Qualities of compassion are patience and wisdom; kindness and perseverance; warmth and resolve. Expression of compassion is prone to be hierarchical, paternalistic and controlling in responses.[124] Just imagine professionals like teachers, doctors, lawyers and politicians exercising compassion in its true form. A patient teacher, a kind doctor, a lawyer who will persevere for a noble cause and a politician who is resolved to do what is right. They are there, but they are few. We need more. Compassion looks beyond the paycheck alone (even though it's important for sustenance) to caring enough for another's predicament.

---

the link between compassion and teacher work engagement. Teaching and Teacher Education, 59, 126-136.

[120] Thompson, B. L., & Waltz, J. (2008). Self-compassion and PTSD symptom severity. Journal of Traumatic Stress: Official Publication of The International Society for Traumatic Stress Studies, 21(6), 556-558.

[121] Phillips, W. J., & Ferguson, S. J. (2013). Self-compassion: A resource for positive aging. Journals of Gerontology Series B: Psychological Sciences and Social Sciences, 68(4), 529-539.

[122] Neff, K. D. (2011). Self-compassion, self-esteem, and well-being. Social and personality psychology compass, 5(1), 1-12.

[123] Allen, A. B., & Leary, M. R. (2010). Self-Compassion, stress, and coping. Social and personality psychology compass, 4(2), 107-118.

[124] Gilbert, P. (2010). The Compassionate Mind: A New Approach to Life's Challenges. constable.

We can simply argue that the difference between compassion and empathy is that compassion goes a step further by showing the intention to help and not just the ability to take the perspective of and feel the emotions of another person. This means empathy precedes compassion. Empathy without compassion leaves the individual drained of energy as a result of feeling what the other feels. There are several types of empathy[125]:

1. Cognitive empathy is also known as "perspective-taking". It is not really what most of us would think of as empathy at all. It is defined by knowing, understanding, or comprehending on an intellectual level. Cognitive empathy is essentially being able to put yourself into someone else's place, and seeing their perspective. It is a useful skill, particularly in negotiations. Cognitive empathy is about thought, as most of us know. To understand pain is not the same thing as feeling pain. So, it would be easy for me to tell someone: "I understand your pain," and do nothing to help the person.
2. Emotional Empathy is also known as "personal distress" or "emotional contagion". Just like it sounds, it includes directly feeling the emotions of another. This is closer to the usual understanding of the word "empathy", but more emotional. It implies a person with the ability to fully take on

---

[125] Spitz, E. R. (2021). The Three Kinds of Empathy: Emotional, Cognitive, Compassionate. Heartmanity. Retrieved August 2, 2020, from https://blog.heartmanity.com/the-three-kinds-of-empathy-emotional-cognitive-compassionate

the emotional and mental state of another. So, it would still be easy for me to tell someone: "I understand and feel your pain," and do nothing to help the person.
3. Compassionate empathy is consistent with what we usually understand by compassion. Like sympathy, compassion is about feeling concern for someone but with an additional move towards action to alleviate the problem. Compassionate empathy is the type of empathy that is usually most appropriate. When you are compassionate, you feel the pain of another, and then you do what you can to alleviate the person's suffering.

Most of the time, compassionate empathy is ideal. Cognitive empathy may be suitable for the workplace, financial negotiations or doctor's offices; Emotional empathy can be the first reaction with cute pets, children and for our loved ones generally; Compassionate empathy strikes an equilibrium between the two. It calls to you to be the solution to the problem of your fellow human. Instead of just saying, "what a pity", or "how sad", it calls you to get up and do something. It is not just about feeling or understanding; it is about action: doing something to help that person out. What I am trying to point out in this chapter is that compassion is important and it calls for actions not just words or feelings. You cannot tell a hungry person, "I'll pray for you", when you can actually buy them food. Buying food for that person is compassion, not praying for them; praying for them is to tell them you understand to make yourself feel good about yourself.

That said, it is important to acknowledge that compassion has three dimensions: receiving compassion, self-compassion, and extending compassion. At different points in our lives, we might find ourselves in one or more of these three dimensions. It is always important that the Golden Rule is a gauge and a guide when dealing with people[126]. The Golden Rule is the principle of treating others as you want to be treated. It is a maxim that is enshrined in many religions and cultures across the world. It can be considered as ethics of reciprocity. The good news is that compassion can be taught and learnt at all stages: early childhood,[127] older children,[128] professionals[129] and adults of every age.[130] Dr. Rankin, a physician and New York Times bestselling author, gave ten ways to cultivate compassion[131]:

1. Practicing self-compassion – you cannot give what you do not have.
2. Put yourself in someone else's shoes – see it from others' view point.
3. Move beyond your self-referencing – don't just think about yourself; it's not all about you.
4. Practice kindness, without people-pleasing – do it because it is the right thing to do.

---

[126]Armstrong, K. (2011). A Charter for Compassion. Religions, (1), 21.
[127]Jalongo, M. R. (2014). Teaching compassion: Humane education in early childhood. Springer.
[128]Levine, D. A. (2013). Teaching empathy: A blueprint for caring, compassion, and community. Solution Tree Press.
[129]Germer, C., & Neff, K. (2019). Teaching the mindful self-compassion program: A guide for professionals. Guilford Publications.
[130]Allen, A. B., Goldwasser, E. R., & Leary, M. R. (2012). Self-compassion and well-being among older adults. Self and Identity, 11(4), 428-453.
[131]Rankin, L. (2020, April 8). 10 Easy Ways to Cultivate Compassion. Mindbodygreen. https://www.mindbodygreen.com/0-23406/10-easy-ways-to-cultivate-compassion.html

5. Relax your judgments – nobody is perfect; not even you.
6. Listen generously – truly listen to understand and not just to plan a response.
7. Heal your own trauma – face your "demons" so they don't undermine you. Bitter and indifferent people can't exercise compassion.
8. Practice presence – giving your full and undivided attention at that place, at that moment, to that person.
9. Practice radical self-care – replenish yourself by taking care of yourself in order to be in a state of mind to have compassion for others.
10. Try the compassion challenge – challenge yourself to be compassionate for a day, a week, a month, a year and forever.

Compassion gives us the aptitude to understand someone else's situation and the yearning to take action to improve their lives. It is a fact that our society cannot function without compassion. It's an essential part of our relationships, families, and communities. Compassion is needed to guarantee that all those in need get the support and services they require. Compassion energizes society to be inclusive and to allow all of its members to be fully engaged in a vibrant life. By practicing compassion as Africans, we express the true idea of ubuntu and how we truly are connected on several levels. In the words of Archbishop Desmond Tutu, "Africans have a thing called ubuntu. We believe that a person is a person through other persons. That my humanity is caught up, bound up, inextricably, with yours. When I dehumanize you, I dehumanize myself. The solitary human being is a contradiction in terms. Therefore, you seek to work for the common good because your humanity comes into its own in community, in belonging." I personally believe that not having compassion for a fellow human is dehumanizing that person and ourselves as ubuntu suggests.[132] It is an obligation to find it in ourselves to relieve another person's suffering.

---

[132] Louw, D. J. (2006). The African concept of Ubuntu. Handbook of restorative justice: A global perspective, 161-174.

Humility

> "A great man is always willing to be little."
> **Ralph Waldo Emerson**

> "There is nothing noble in being superior to your fellow men. True nobility lies in being superior to your former self."
> **Ernest Hemingway**

> "You cannot be truly humble, unless you truly believe that life can and will go on without you."
> **Mokokoma Mokhonoana**

Though humility has long been regarded as a virtue in most cultures and religions, humility is no longer a popular quality in the world and in the continent of Africa[133]. From musicians showing off their "bling" in music videos to the average African getting loans to throw extravagant parties they can't afford; humility appears to be dead. It is perceived as a sign of weakness or powerlessness. The belief is that if you have it, then flaunt it. So, when someone appears to be humble, the belief is that that person is broke, powerless and in need of a favour. In the African society, it is not uncommon for people you meet to try to let you know in your first few minutes of encounter how important they are, by stating people they know, who knows someone very important and how they are not as simple as they appear to look. This is because in Africa, if you are not important, people will not take you seriously and one perception of showing importance is a lack of humility. When people want to take advantage of others or abuse their position, they make the comment: "do you know who I am?" Strangely even people who are nobodies use the phrase as a basis to intimidate and oppress others. The dislike for humility has even gone as far as people perceiving humble people as innately arrogant. This is due to the fact that humble people who have power, position and accolade tend to ignore disrespectful and arrogant people and are perceived as being aloof by the said group of people. In Africa, probably like everywhere else, you will find poor people, religious people, educated people, political leaders[134] and people from

---

[133]Lynch, M. P. (2017). Teaching humility in an age of arrogance. Chronicle Review, B10-B11.
[134]Nolen, S. (2008, March 13). S. African leaders 'corrupt, arrogant,' Tutu says. The Globe and Mail. https://www.theglobeandmail.com/news/world/s-african-leaders-corrupt-arrogant-tutu-says/article17981975/

different walks of life who lack any sense of humility.

Humility is not modesty[135]. Humility is derived from the Latin word *humus* which means "earth" or "dirt", while modesty is derived from the Latin word *modus* which implies "manner" or "measure", and implies restraint in appearance and behavior. In other words, modesty is simply the unwillingness to flaunt, display, or otherwise draw attention to oneself, which in most cases is related to context. For example, when people go to the church or mosque, they tend to be modest, but that does not necessarily mean they are humble. This can be proven by their conduct in everyday life.

Humility is often characterized as genuine gratitude and a lack of arrogance: a modest view of one's self (as opposed to presenting it to others). The definition of humility is the feeling or attitude that you have no special importance that makes you better than others or having a lack of pride. While being humble necessitates recognizing our own flaws, inadequacies, and limits, it doesn't mean making a show of them. It is important to note that humility shouldn't be misunderstood as low self-esteem, timidity, feelings of inferiority, or self-degradation; they are not the same as humility. Humility is not about belittling yourself by downplaying your remarkable qualities and achievements; it is about knowing that in spite of your remarkable qualities and achievement you do not feel you are entitled to special treatment[136]. A truly humble person will understand that

---

[135] Davis, D. E., McElroy, S. E., Rice, K. G., Choe, E., Westbrook, C., Hook, J. N., ... & Worthington Jr, E. L. (2016). Is modesty a subdomain of humility?. The Journal of Positive Psychology, 11(4), 439-446.

their achievement does not make them superior to others because that sense of superiority is a distraction to what can make them even better. It eliminates the room for improvement and personal development.

Humility is one of the most powerful and important attributes of growth in life. It is argued that humility is an indicator of psychological and spiritual maturity, and internal confidence. Being humble helps to build trust and facilitates learning, which are key aspects of leadership and personal development[137]. It is a fact that some great thinkers and philosophers don't think much of humility, from Aristotle not including it in the list of virtues to David Hume and Friedrich Nietzsche condemning it. Hume referred to it as part of the "monkish virtues"[138] and Nietzsche categorized it as part of "Slave morality". In fact, Nietzsche believed that humility was a hinderance to humanity's progress[139]. However, several other thinkers beg to disagree. Nelson Mandela pointed out the importance of humility: "The first thing is to be honest with yourself. You can never have an impact on society if you have not changed yourself... Great peacemakers are all people of integrity, of honesty, but humility." What Mandela seems to have pointed out is intellectual humility. Studies have also

---

[136]Banker, C. C., & Leary, M. R. (2020). Hypo-egoic nonentitlement as a feature of humility. Personality and Social Psychology Bulletin, 46(5), 738-753.
[137]Owens, B. P., Johnson, M. D., & Mitchell, T. R. (2013). Expressed humility in organizations: Implications for performance, teams, and leadership. Organization Science, 24(5), 1517-1538.
[138]Davie, W. (1999). Hume on monkish virtues. Hume studies, 25(1/2), 139-153.
[139]Bollinger, R. A., & Hill, P. C. (2012). Humility. In T. G. Plante (Ed.), Religion, spirituality, and positive psychology: Understanding the psychological fruits of faith (p. 31–47). Praeger/ABC-CLIO.

backed the positive effects of humility especially in strengthening social bonds and better health outcomes among others.[140]

Humility allows one to see beyond themselves and to be more open to others' views and ideas. Intellectual humility is often described as an intellectual virtue along with other perceived virtues such as open-mindedness, intellectual courage and integrity. Intellectual humility has been recognized as a character virtue that allows individuals to recognize their own possible unreliability when forming and adjusting attitudes. Intellectual humility is therefore vital for avoiding confirmation biases when reasoning[141]. Confirmation bias is simply the fact that we tend to see or notice evidence that supports what we want to believe and this of course is not objective. This bias has a substantial effect on the appropriate functioning of society by misrepresenting evidence-based decision-making which can result in maintenance of several prejudices (e.g., tribalism, sexism, etc.). Researchers are inclined to believe that intellectual humility is better for people than intellectual arrogance and closed-mindedness and that intellectual humility advances well-being, enhances tolerance for other perspectives, and promotes inquiry and learning[142].

---

[140]Davis, D. E., & Hook, J. N. (2013). Measuring humility and its positive effects. APS Observer, 26(8).
[141]Zmigrod, L., Zmigrod, S., Rentfrow, P. J., & Robbins, T. W. (2019). The psychological roots of intellectual humility: The role of intelligence and cognitive flexibility. Personality and Individual Differences, 141, 200-208.
[142]Leary, M. R., Diebels, K. J., Davisson, E. K., Jongman-Sereno, K. P., Isherwood, J. C., Raimi, K. T., ... & Hoyle, R. H. (2017). Cognitive and interpersonal features of intellectual humility. Personality and Social Psychology Bulletin, 43(6), 793-813.

Intellectual humility is a result of a growth mindset. Stanford psychologist, Carol Dweck identified two types of mindsets that people possess[143]: the growth and the fixed mindsets. In a fixed mindset, people believe their qualities are stagnant traits and therefore cannot change. People with a fixed mindset believe they are born with their abilities which are fixed and unalterable, creating a glass ceiling for their success that they can never exceed. These people show off their intelligence and talents instead of working to enhance and improve them. They also believe that talent solely leads to success, and effort is not a necessity. On the other hand, in a growth mindset, people have a fundamental belief that their learning and intelligence can grow over time and with experience. People with a growth mindset believe their abilities can be developed and strengthened over time through hard work and commitment. When people accept that they can become smarter, they understand that their effort has an impact on their success, so they put in more time, practice and learning, leading to higher achievement. They have no glass ceilings to limit what they can achieve. People with growth mindsets see failures as an opportunity to learn, to review and to do better next time. Without humility and intellectual humility, we are people with a fixed mindset who believe that we are who we are and nothing can be done about it. I personally believe that a fixed mindset is a prison that people lock themselves in and it hinders them from bettering themselves and realizing their full potential. It creates the type of people who say, "I am too old", "I am

---

[143] Dweck, C. S. (2008). Mindset: The new psychology of success. Random House Digital, Inc.

too young", "I just can't...", etc. In Africa, we need people with a growth mindset who are not afraid of failing or looking silly because they know that at the end of it all, they will rise and come forth as gold. As a person, a parent, a teacher, a leader or anyone in any sphere of society, having a growth mindset will always make the difference. A society filled with people who have growth mindsets will prioritize learning and education.

A point to note is that we can actually move from one mindset to the other, depending on what task we are trying to attempt or don't want to attempt is. So, it has to be a deliberate choice to capture yourself when shifting to a fixed mindset on a matter. The website, "Develop Good Habits" gives strategies on developing a growth mindset, and they include[144]:

1. Recognize and embrace your weaknesses so that you can try to improve.
2. Perceive challenges as opportunities to learn and grow.
3. Know your learning style and use the right learning strategies.
4. Remember that the brain has the ability to change throughout life.
5. Prioritize learning over seeking approval. Knowledge over certificates.
6. Focus on the process instead of the end result. Skills over accomplishment.

---

[144] Develop Good Habits. (2020, June 5). Fixed Mindset vs. Growth Mindset: What REALLY Matters for Success. https://www.developgoodhabits.com/fixed-mindset-vs-growth-mindset/

7. Cultivate a sense of purpose. What you want to achieve.
8. Choose learning well over learning fast. Quality over quantity.
9. Reward effort and actions, not traits. It's how hard you try that matters.
10. Learn to give and receive constructive criticism. It will only make you better.
11. Need for improvement does not mean failure. You can always do better.
12. Reflect on your learning every day. Take inventory of your growth.
13. Learn from the mistakes of others. Experience is a cruel teacher.
14. Think of learning as "brain training." Exercise your brain.
15. Cultivate grit to stay motivated and focused. Cling to the dream/vision.
16. Never stop learning. Set a new goal for every one you accomplished.
17. Remember that it takes time to learn. Be patient with yourself.

As mentioned earlier, in order to develop a growth mindset, you must be willing to commit to changing your beliefs about what you are able to do. You have to believe that your talents and abilities are not inborn but are a result of the effort that you put in. Yes, some people are naturally talented but if they don't put in the effort, then they end up not achieving their greatest potential. No matter how good or bad you are, you can always improve yourself. All you have to do is put in the effort.

It is a fact that many leaders are outright arrogant and the word humility does not register anywhere close to their name. This raises the question of whether a leader has any need for humility. Confidence is good in leaders, but not arrogance. Similarly, humility is an exceptional leadership trait, not modesty. A 2014 study[145] focusing on humility as a key leadership trait among successful leaders stated that: "Humility is manifested in self-awareness, openness to feedback, appreciation of others, low self-focus, and pursuit of self-transcendence. Humble people willingly seek accurate self-knowledge and accept their imperfections while remaining fully aware of their talents and abilities. They appreciate others' positive worth, strengths, and contributions and thus have no need for entitlement or dominance over others."[146]

Sadly, in Africa, we have no shortage of leaders who are arrogant, from business leaders to political leaders.[147] Psychologist, Cherrie Campbell,[148] gave reasons why humility is a profound ingredient to exceptional leadership:

---

[145]Ou, A. Y., Tsui, A. S., Kinicki, A. J., Waldman, D. A., Xiao, Z., & Song, L. J. (2014). Humble chief executive officers' connections to top management team integration and middle managers' responses. Administrative Science Quarterly, 59(1), 34-72.
[146]Nielsen, D. (2022). Humility's Role in Leadership. Retrieved 9 March 2022, from https://www.jhconline.com/humilitys-role-in-leadership.html
[147]Bennett-Jones, O. (2015, July 13). The arrogance of power. BBC News. https://www.bbc.com/news/world-33475303
[148]Campbell, S. (2017, August 24). 9 Reasons Humility Is the Key Ingredient to Exceptional Leadership. Entrepreneur. https://www.entrepreneur.com/article/299140

1. A healthy sense of humility is essential to great leadership due to the fact that it authenticates a person's humanity.
2. Humble leaders use their position as a means to encourage others, and to delegate authority and responsibility to those capable of doing the work; they do not use rank as a basis to abuse or exploit others.
3. Those who lead from a humility perspective understand that the best way to prepare their team for success is to encourage, support and promote their team to believe in their own potential for success.
4. Humble leaders focus on the strength of their team members and acknowledge them with an unwavering belief.
5. Collaborative leadership views team membership from a place of equality, with each possessing their own set of skills.
6. When being led from humility, team members know that losing one battle is not indicative of losing the war; it is simply a learning experience.
7. Leaders who possess humility have developed this character trait through much success and much suffering which helps them develop into resilient, intuitive, hard-working, and incredibly experienced people.
8. Leaders who operate from humility did not build their reputation on a set of fictional, loud, and flashy pretenses; they built it on a reputation of integrity.
9. The most impactful way to lead others is to be mindful of inclusion, and in the elimination of

prejudices; those who lead with humility welcome differences.

It is my belief that the higher you rise in life, career and achievement, the more humility one should practice in order to grow even more and rise even higher. In my book, *the life of Another One*, I wrote about "never reaching the peak, but always being close to it"[149], it simply implies always knowing you can do better, you can learn much more and you can definitely grow more. Never ever feel that you have arrived. Never retire from trying to achieve and inspire through humility to learn something new in order to be an even better person.

---

[149]Osunsan, O.K. (2010). *The Life of Another One*. CreateSpace

Loyalty

"Within the hearts of men, loyalty and consideration are esteemed greater than success."
Bryant H. McGill

"Loyalty is the strongest glue which makes a relationship last for a life time."
Mario Puzo

"The test of good citizenship is loyalty to country."
Bainbridge Colby

Loyalty is a magnificent thing in action and it has been the inspiration behind some of the greatest stories ever told. Loyalty represents commitment and dedication to another enabling respect and trust to flourish. To be loyal is to be a person that anybody can trust; that trust guarantees that you will act in the interest of the person you are loyal to. It is defined as devotion and faithfulness to a nation, cause, philosophy, country, group, or person. When you ask many people if they are loyal, they will probably say "yes" and that might be true. It depends on what one is loyal to; from the egoistic perspective of self to the altruistic perspective of others, loyalty can take different shapes, forms, and sizes. The type of loyalty I want to focus on in this chapter is that type that calls for altruism. This type of loyalty is not truly appreciated in the modern world we live in, in spite of the significance it has on all our lives. Loyalty anchors our personal to professional relationships and without it, the quality of life is questionable.

In spite of celebrating loyalty as one of the greatest traits an amazing person should possess in relationships, be it romantic, friendship, business, or otherwise; people do not always reciprocate it. Thus, we have cheaters, frenemies and job-hoppers. Modern society does not necessarily feel loyalty is a big deal. Our modern world calls for us to be sharp, shrewd and ready to protect our own interest in order to survive and thrive. This belief suggests that loyalty is conditional, temporary and has to have an element of personal interest. Interestingly, loyalty is the virtue that can end all of the problems of human society. It is argued that the world has moved from a society of long-term relationships to a society of transactional transient relationships. It is argued to be the result of the flexible and more mobile lifestyles we adopt, which has made businesses and some people wealthier at the cost of being less loyal.[150]

The fact is that loyalty cannot be bought or sold; it must be earned and nurtured over time. It is not a short-term undertaking; it is the understanding of the big picture and what is at stake. It should never be undermined or taken advantage of. Loyalty is a form of currency that all parties will often times draw upon in times of need or crisis. It is a fact that loyalty typifies a person in virtue of some relational role: a husband is loyal to his wife; an employee to his employer; a citizen to his country. These relationships don't have to be totally exclusive in that a person may be loyal to all his friends; a customer to all his vendors. It's not possible for a person to be loyal to everyone. This is because a person cannot be loyal to his friends and to their adversaries; he cannot be loyal to his vendors and to their competitors. That becomes a conflict of interest; in other words, disloyalty[151]. The point I am trying to make is that as a person, you have to choose who and what to be loyal to because who or what you are loyal to defines you as a person. The same can be said about what you are disloyal to. Loyalty plays an essential role in our identities.[152] Being loyal is a good thing. In fact, studies have suggested that being loyal is beneficial, especially in romantic relationships due to the fact that it reduces illness and enhances vitality and longevity.[153]

---

[150]Keiningham, T., Aksoy, L., & Williams, L. (2010). Why Loyalty Matters: The Groundbreaking Approach to Rediscovering Happiness, Meaning, and Lasting Fulfillment in Your Life and Work. ReadHowYouWant. com.
[151]Donway, R. (2013, January 13). The Moral Tradition: The Concept of Loyalty. The Atlas Society. https://atlassociety.org/commentary/commentary-blog/5153-the-moral-tradition-the-concept-of-loyalty-
[152]Fletcher, G. (1993). Loyalty. Theological Studies, 54, 766-766.
[153]Wang, S. S. (2011, June 21). The Health Benefits of Staying Loyal. WSJ.

In leadership and government, being loyal to a leader will result in a better society. When each member of the society is loyal to the leadership, it's easier to enforce laws, rules and regulations. The leader can trust his subordinates to be people of integrity so that he can achieve his goals for the country. Loyalty is needed everywhere. Loyalty is a necessity in family relationships and friendships; it is also the basis for commitments to others in social or civic relationships[154]. This means, loyal members of groups are expected to put the interests of their group ahead of those of other groups. Group loyalty, which is loyalty that goes beyond an individual to a collection of others who may identify with each other on the basis of similarities,[155] is needed in Africa for Africa. We need to see our country and continent as an extension of ourselves and who we are and when it fails, we have failed[156]. This means, we need to be more altruistic in our obligation to our country and countrymen and women. This attachment should be so well woven into our identity that when we act in the interest (sacrifice for) of our country, countrymen and women, we feel we are acting in our own self-interest[157]. The term "faithfulness to obligations" has been linked to the concept of loyalty[158]. I believe that as Africans we have to be faithful in our obligations to our country and

---

https://www.wsj.com/articles/SB10001424052702304887904576397801582783690

[154] Felten, E. (2011). Loyalty: The vexing virtue. Simon and Schuster.
[155] Fletcher, G. (1993). Loyalty. Theological Studies, 54, 33-34.
[156] Jollimore, T. A. (2013). On loyalty. Routledge.
[157] Jollimore, T. A. (2013). On loyalty. Routledge, p.16.
[158] Bryant, S. (1915). Loyalty. James Hasting's Encyclopaedia of Religion and Ethics, 8, 183-188.

continent; we have to do what is right; we have to be loyal. We have to be patriotic. We have to be patriotic because when all is said and done, we are all related, you just have to travel far back enough. We have to be patriotic because it enlarges our lives and it helps us defend and protect our identity. Being patriotic does not imply being a nationalist[159] but it does mean putting the interest of your country first like any other responsible citizen would but not to the exclusion or detriment of the interests of other nations.[160]

So, what does patriotism mean? Along with deep-seated love, patriotism is the feeling of pride, devotion, and attachment to a homeland, as well as a feeling of attachment to other patriotic citizens of the said homeland. It means you don't have to be on the African continent to be patriotic. As long as Africa is your homeland and you love it, you are a patriot. Loving your country means working to make the country better for the greater good and the generations to come, by obeying the laws, paying your taxes and speaking up to make your voice heard when the need arises, among other things. You cannot be a patriot and pollute or disrespect your country and fellow citizens because you feel you are well-travelled or more educated. Definitely, corruption and patriotism do not go together and of course, supporting your national team is not the only act of patriotism required of you. It means the government officials put the interest of the citizens first and not

---

[159]Viroli, M. (1995). For love of country: An essay on patriotism and nationalism. Clarendon Press.
[160]Dictionary.com. (2020, April 17). "Patriotism" vs. "Nationalism": What's the Difference? https://www.dictionary.com/e/patriotism-vs-nationalism/

personal interest; it means politicians are loyal to the people who gave them the mandate; and it means institutions are considerate to people who have given of themselves to make the institution work. We need to reinforce the need to be loyal at every level of society, so that by the time people get to the post of authority they still understand what it means to be loyal. I can be bold enough to say that if you are loyal to yourself, your family, your community and country, then you are patriotic. Being loyal implies sticking with it even when things don't look good. This can apply to relationships and of course countries. It is easy to be loyal when you feel your government is efficient, your team is winning or the relationship is in the high. True loyalty is tested when more is asked of you than is given to you. Again, I will repeat that no one is perfect, but that is not an excuse not to try. If every African makes an effort to be loyal and patriotic, there will be a positive transformative revolution on the continent. It is a simple matter of choice. Do not self-sellout.

Selflessness

"Teach all men to fish, but first teach all men to be fair. Take less, give more. Give more of yourself, take less from the world. Nobody owes you anything, you owe the world everything."
Suzy Kassem

Only those who have learned the power of sincere and selfless contribution experience life's deepest joy: true fulfillment.
Tony Robbins

"Nothing liberates our greatness like the desire to help, the desire to serve."
Marianne Williamson

Selflessness is an imperative in marriage, friendships, and most relationships. It is also vital for happiness and fulfillment in life. Research has confirmed that giving one's money or time improves happiness and psychological well-being.[161] We now live in a world where service and selflessness are almost seen as naive and unwise. We ascribe importance and worth to people who accumulate wealth and riches in their unquenching quest for more. We sometimes villainize people who selflessly think for the good of society and act in ways that foster humanity. Children are taught in school and at home how it is so important to be wealthy and accumulate wealth instead of working towards the betterment of society that will produce a better quality of life. Like the fictional character Gordon Gekko, we are told "greed is good" and it implies ambition and the drive to succeed. Motivational speakers imply it and even some prosperity preachers endorse it. What is the point of wealth if it does not improve the quality of life of the owner and those around him or her? Now the quality of life has little to do with wealth and that is why we have wealthy people who have given up on life. Wealth, however, can help enhance the quality of life if it is used wisely. Sadly, some people's goal in life is to be wealthy and that is it; wealth without purpose can become a burden. A cynic would argue that it is better to be wealthy without a purpose than to be poor with a purpose. That is a matter of debate but being wealthy

---

[161]Dunn, E. W., Aknin, L. B., & Norton, M. I. (2014). Prosocial spending and happiness: Using money to benefit others pays off. Current Directions in Psychological Science, 23(1), 41-47.

without a purpose is an indication of a lack of wisdom. One of my favorite authors, Khalil Gibran, stated that "wisdom ceases to be wisdom when it becomes too proud to weep, too grave to laugh, and too selfish to seek other than itself." Being wealthy without a purpose is selfish.

Conceptualizing or defining selflessness can be complicated. Some will even argue that true selflessness is impossible because even if we are doing something for somebody without expectations of a reward, we still gain something; the feeling of having done good. This feeling can give us a sense of worth at times. Selflessness is giving of your time, money, resources and effort. Selflessness is acting without thinking about how we will profit, benefit or be rewarded. If we help others, but expect recognition or the favour to be returned, this is not a selfless action. True selflessness means we would engage in an act of kindness, even if it is never known to anyone else. Selflessness implies we have compassion on others. This service to others is not a gesture of patronizing charity in helping others; our action is inspired by a feeling of compassion and obligation. Selflessness is about identifying with problems and suffering of others. Selflessness is very hard for a lot of people to practice because in truth, we all have problems and the question is what makes my problem less important than that of others? Willingness to focus on others in spite of one's own problems, issues and limitations is what make selflessness such a remarkable quality.

Selflessness is habitually ignored as a conduit to happiness for the reason that, on the surface, it seems to conflict with the very notion of happiness. The benefits of selflessness in the form of giving have been documented by research and it always points to the fact that it can help decrease the symptoms of depression and anxiety[162], and improves positive moods[163], and all-round happiness[164] across all age ranges. It can also increase happiness as stated earlier, life satisfaction, self-esteem, and mastery over time[165,166]. It is safe to say that selflessness is its own reward.

Our lives can be lived for several purposes. They can be applied to advance our personal ambitions to acquire money, possessions, fame, prestige, or reputation. We, however, have the choice to live our lives in the pursuit of justice, happiness, or growth for another person or groups of people. As an African, live to solve the issues we encounter on this continent and in this world. We can dedicate ourselves to advancing the ideals that will create a better country and continent by embracing service and selflessness. This does not mean that you overlook yourself and your wellbeing; it means you look out for the interest of others as well.

---

[162]Crocker, J., Canevello, A., Breines, J. G., & Flynn, H. (2010). Interpersonal goals and change in anxiety and dysphoria in first-semester college students. Journal of personality and social psychology, 98(6), 1009.

[163]Yinon, Y., & Landau, M. O. (1987). On the reinforcing value of helping behavior in a positive mood. Motivation and Emotion, 11(1), 83-93.

[164]Aknin, L. B., Hamlin, J. K., & Dunn, E. W. (2012). Giving leads to happiness in young children. PLoS one, 7(6), e39211.

[165]Musick, M. A., & Wilson, J. (2003). Volunteering and depression: The role of psychological and social resources in different age groups. Social science & medicine, 56(2), 259-269.

[166]Thoits PA, Hewitt LN. 2001. Volunteer work and well-being. J. Health Soc. Behav. 42: 115–31

As leaders, we have the obligation to serve and be selfless because at the core of true leadership is service[167]. In other words, to be a leader, a parent, a manager, a member of parliament, a president or whichever capacity, you need to have been inspired by the desire to serve people; to be selfless. We need leaders who offer themselves to serve; not to rule, dominate or oppress people. You don't need to search too far to know that we have more than our share of selfish leaders in Africa[168]. Fela Anikulapo Kuti, the Nigerian Afrobeat maestro, claimed we have Vagabonds in Power (VIP) in Africa[169]. These VIPs have placed Africans in fetters, rags and reduced them to beggars. It is argued that the leadership crisis that continues to plague the African continent is a result of African leaders not seeing themselves as part of the people they lead: they operate within cabals that are driven by selfishness to the enrichment of the ruling elites.[170] This implies a lack of empathy and compassion for the people they lead due to the fact that they are so far cut off from them and are unable to relate to their plight. The Chairperson of the African Union Commission, Dr Nkosazana Dlamini-Zuma, pointed out this selfishness

---

[167]Taylor, T., Martin, B. N., Hutchinson, S., & Jinks, M. (2007). Examination of leadership practices of principals identified as servant leaders. International journal of leadership in education, 10(4), 401-419.

[168]Nsehe, M. (2012, February 11). The Five Worst Leaders in Africa. Forbes. https://www.forbes.com/sites/mfonobongnsehe/2012/02/09/the-five-worst-leaders-in-africa/

[169]Mbamalu, S. (2019, September 26). Vagabonds in Power (V.I.P.): Africa's greatest problem is selfish leadership. This Is Africa. https://thisisafrica.me/politics-and-society/vagabonds-in-power-africas-leadership-problem/

[170]Mbamalu, S. (2019, September 26). Vagabonds in Power (V.I.P.): Africa's greatest problem is selfish leadership. This Is Africa. https://thisisafrica.me/politics-and-society/vagabonds-in-power-africas-leadership-problem/

and how governments and leaders in the continent are causing the suffering of their people. She was quoted as saying: "Our governments and leadership are there to protect the vulnerable, to serve the people, and not to be the cause of the people's suffering and retrogression... Enough is enough. Africans deserve better, and we must all work towards better days, and towards peace, stability and development".[171] It is a tragedy that a continent of wealth in terms of natural resources is so poor in terms of leadership and vision[172]. It is a known fact that selfish leaders are usually afraid of two things. The fear of being exposed as incompetent and the fact that they are unwilling and unable to make the same sacrifices they demand of others.

Over the years, Africans have sacrificed a lot. The new generation of African leaders need to know that they have to make the sacrifices too in solidity with the people they lead. Why should a leader send his children to study abroad when he is responsible for the mess in the educational system in his country? Why should his wife be flown abroad to seek medical attention when his fellow citizens are stuck with a failed health system? Why should he live in such opulence when most of the tax payers are living hand to mouth? Why? It is because Africa's problems are not just the fault of leaders, in fact it is mostly the fault of the armchair politicians, philosophers, and critics who have failed to do their part.

---

[171]ANA-CAJ. (2017, January 3). Dlamini-Zuma lambasts "selfish" African leaders. IOL. https://www.iol.co.za/news/africa/dlamini-zuma-lambasts-selfish-african-leaders-7319589

[172]War on Want. (2015, December 22). Africa: A continent of wealth, a continent of poverty. https://waronwant.org/media/africa-continent-wealth-continent-poverty

If you feel you can do better, get up and get involved in building your country: be the voice of reason, be the change you want to see. You don't have to be the president to change the destiny of a nation. You can change the nation by being selfless in your capacity as a parent, a teacher, a lawyer, a doctor, a cleaner or any other sphere you operate in as a person. Your selflessness will be an inspiration to others; it will challenge them to be better and to do better. It will make them selfless too and as you look out for their interest, they will look out for yours. It will take time but it works. Do your research; selfless people from the likes of mother Theresa to Nelson Mandela have changed the world. Truly, selflessness can change the world[173] and definitely Africa. It has before and it can again.[174] Be a selfless African.

---

[173] Pearson, F. (2014). Secret kindness agents: How small acts of kindness really can change the world. BQB Publishing.
[174] Grimes, A. C. (2016, December 29). 10 Selfless Heroes Who Made the World A Happier Place. Listverse. https://listverse.com/2016/12/29/10-selfless-heroes-who-made-the-world-a-happier-place/

Enterprising

"To be happy at home is the ultimate result of all ambition, the end to which every enterprise and labor tends, and of which every desire prompts the prosecution."
Samuel Johnson

"Be prepared to sacrifice, and work harder than you've ever thought possible. Be prepared to work around the clock, to be laughed at, called a dreamer, and to be told several times that your ideas will not work."
Nkemdilim Begho

"The West has taken and borrowed a lot from Africa…now it's a renaissance: we're claiming back

what is ours and we're adding value to what is ours, making it globally acceptable and globally appealing."
Deola Sagoe

Africans are not lazy; they are just tired of being exploited and disenfranchised. Some of the hardest working people in the world live on the continent of Africa. They range from the child who hawks produce to contribute to the family income, the mother who wakes up first and goes to bed last and the man who spends the whole day doing manual labour. These indicators might not appear in the publications used to access productivity, but these people spend hours upon hours toiling to itch out a living off the fat of barren land. Yes, they may not be working smart as we like to put it now, but they are definitely hard workers. If given the opportunity, they can work smart and be much more productive.

According to Jim Rohn, "an enterprising person is one who comes across a pile of scrap metal and sees the making of a wonderful sculpture. An enterprising person is one who drives through an old decrepit part of town and sees a new housing development. An enterprising person is one who sees opportunity in all areas of life. To be enterprising is to keep your eyes open and your mind active. It's to be skilled enough, confident enough, creative enough and disciplined enough to seize opportunities that present themselves…regardless of the economy."[175] Being enterprising is a mindset. An

---

[175] Rohn, J. (2002). Creating opportunity. E-Zine Journal, 22, 116.

enterprising mindset is about having a way of thinking which sees opportunities and possibilities instead of limitations and failures. A person with an enterprising mindset wants to make a difference instead of complaining about the prevailing situation. This mindset is not limited to businesses, entrepreneurs or money-making, it is the same mindset that has influenced people to usher in social good and transform their societies. The enterprising mindset can be beneficial to society in several ways. I believe this mindset is embodied by a lot of Africans. This is so in spite of the limitations in some African countries where the political, economic, legal and even social systems have failed[176]. You will still find the resilience of the African people rising like dust, in spite of being stomped on. You will see them rise like smoke in spite of their aspirations being burnt down. Africans are resilient and enterprising; they make the most of inhabitable conditions.[177] They always try to find a way.

Every year, thousands of Africans travel abroad in search of a better future. Many start out doing menial jobs but through social mobility, they rise through their children and children's children to become exceptional people who change national destinies. They become the next Barrack Obama, Giannis Sina Ugo Antetokounmpo, Trevor Noah, Tidjane Thiam and Elon Musks. Africans have always thrived and even excelled when given equal footing and opportunities as their contemporaries. It has

---

[176]Mazrui, A. A. (1995). The blood of experience: The failed state and political collapse in Africa. World Policy Journal, 12(1), 28-34.
[177]Cooke, J. G. (2015). The state of African resilience: Understanding dimensions of vulnerability and adaptation. Rowman & Littlefield.

been confirmed that African immigrants to countries like the USA are more educated[178] and tend to register remarkable success compared to their contemporaries. This shows that if the atmosphere to excel was created and the possibility of social upward mobility truly existed for all Africans, the continent would not be the same[179]. This tragedy is of course not solely the making of the government but they do have a major role in allowing it to fester[180]. This fact is confirmed with the knowledge that absolute mobility is predominantly low in African economies due to the fact that on average, only 35 percent of adults born in the 1980s have surpassed their parents' educational attainments in comparison to the 60 percent in the high-income economies[181]. These statistics might be an indicator that there is a lack of meritocracy in Africa. The blight of nepotism, cronyism and tribalism has undermined the ability of people to truly excel on the basis of their hard work, effort and merit[182]. Those who truly have the drive to make something of themselves try by any means necessary as a desperate measure. They throw away values and morality because they discover it

---

[178]Simmons, A. M. (2018). African immigrants are more educated than most—including people born in US. Los Angeles Times, 12.
[179]Narayan, A., Van der Weide, R., Cojocaru, A., Lakner, C., Redaelli, S., Mahler, D. G., ... & Thewissen, S. (2018). Fair Progress?: Economic Mobility Across Generations Around the World. World Bank Publications.
[180]Corcoran, B. (2013, October 3). Governments in Africa fail to reduce poverty despite economic progress. The Irish Times. https://www.irishtimes.com/news/world/africa/governments-in-africa-fail-to-reduce-poverty-despite-economic-progress-1.1549194
[181]Narayan, A., Van der Weide, R., Cojocaru, A., Lakner, C., Redaelli, S., Mahler, D. G., ... & Thewissen, S. (2018). Fair Progress?: Economic Mobility Across Generations Around the World. World Bank Publications.
[182]Olabode, O. (2012, July 18). Tribalism, Nepotism, Cronyism and General Poverty. Daily Post Nigeria. https://dailypost.ng/2012/07/18/tribalism-nepotism-cronyism-general-poverty/

does not work and has no significance in such systems. They bend and break the law and do whatever is necessary because the systems have failed them. They are trafficked abroad or embrace any other illegal and possibly dangerous avenues to get to where they want to be. Their ingenuity and enterprising nature are converted to criminality. The ultimate truth is that we are the product of our environment and the result of our experiences.

We don't lack creativity, innovation or ideas in Africa, we lack the opportunities to be rewarded fairly for our efforts. There may be no jobs, but there is always work to be done.

Moral Courage

"Above all, we must realize that no arsenal, or no weapon in the arsenals of the world, is so formidable as the will and moral courage of free men and women. It is a weapon our adversaries in today's world do not have."
Ronald Reagan

"Few men are willing to brave the disapproval of their fellows, the censure of their colleagues, the wrath of their society. Moral courage is a rarer commodity than bravery in battle or great intelligence. Yet it is the one essential, vital quality for those who seek to change the world which yields most painfully to change."

Robert Kennedy

"I learned that courage was not the absence of fear, but the triumph over it. The brave man is not he who does not feel afraid, but he who conquers that fear."

Nelson Mandela

To change anything, courage is needed. The courage to dream, believe and even take action. The courage to stand up in the face of adversity. The courage to be different. Courage plays a major role in personal growth.[183] To grow as a person you have to act on what is right in spite of your fears; that is courage. Courage, according to Aristotle, is the mean (golden mean) between fear and recklessness. Courage is multifaceted.[184] Courage which is also known as fortitude is a quality that everybody wants; it is an attribute that contributes to good character and tends to enhance a person's ability to earn the respect of others. The Free Dictionary defines courage as "The state or quality of mind or spirit that enables one to face danger, fear, or vicissitudes with self-possession, confidence, and resolution; bravery."[185] Others define courage as the means of exercising confidence when

---

[183]Goud, N. H. (2005). Courage: Its nature and development. The Journal of Humanistic Counseling, Education and Development, 44(1), 102-116.

[184]Woodard, C. R., & Pury, C. L. (2007). The construct of courage: Categorization and measurement. Consulting Psychology Journal: Practice and Research, 59(2), 135.

[185]The Free Dictionary. (n.d.). courage. TheFreeDictionary.Com. Retrieved August 14, 2020, from https://www.thefreedictionary.com/courage

carrying out constructive activities, regardless of the pressure to do otherwise. It is the aptitude to face hardship or challenges without wavering on what is right. According to Dr. Lisa Dungate and Jennifer Armstrong, there are six types of courage[186]:

- **Physical courage.** This is what most people know as courage and it is the willingness to be brave at the risk to self. Physical courage implies the readiness to exercise physical vigor to get things done. In order to be physically courageous, a person needs to be physically fit. This includes developing physical strength, resiliency, and alertness.

- **Social courage.** This is the confidence to challenge the leaders of the society whenever they do wrong, as well as getting them to do what is right. Social courage normally includes the risk of social embarrassment or exclusion, unpopularity or rejection in society or among the leadership. Social courage has inspired people to take several human rights actions to challenge the government even at the expense of their own personal safety. Social courage also includes the willingness to stand against vices in society, such as corruption, female genital mutilation, etc. It takes courage for someone or a group to stand up against such practices in societies where they are prevalent.

---

[186]Lion's Whiskers. (n.d.). Lion's Whiskers: The Six Types of Courage. Retrieved August 14, 2020, from http://www.lionswhiskers.com/p/six-types-of-courage.html

- **Intellectual courage.** This is the inclination to engage with stimulating ideas to question our thinking, and the willingness to risk making mistakes. Intellectual courage calls for contending with problematic or perplexing ideas and asking questions in an attempt to gain understanding. It is inspired by the desire to discern and tell the truth. Our quest for the truth sometimes might lead us to challenge our previously accepted ideas or contradicts the values of our family or cultural group. Intellectual courage is believed to be a core quality needed for the future due to the fact that the intricate problems of the environment, economy, and society will call for unconventional problem-solving and the need to unlearn.

- **Emotional courage.** This is the type of courage that releases us to experience the full range of positive emotions at the peril of also encountering the negative ones. Emotional courage is strongly linked to happiness. It is argued that it is impossible to know happiness without experiencing sadness. To fall in love requires emotional courage to be open and vulnerable to the person you love with the possibility of getting hurt at any point in time.

- **Spiritual courage.** This is the inclination to embrace spiritual faith and belief in getting things done, despite the overwhelming urge of temptation in one's way. It takes spiritual courage to stand by what you believe in even when it is easier to take a short cut, e.g., taking a bribe when you are in dire financial strain. Spiritual courage is accepting that you don't have all the answers but believing that God is in control. This strengthens us when we struggle with questions about faith, purpose, and the meaning of life, either in a religious or nonreligious context. Of course, many people find the basis of this courage in religion but there are also other ways to develop spiritual courage. Spiritual courage means opening ourselves up to our vulnerability and the mysteries of life.

- **Moral courage.** This involves doing the right thing, principally at the risk of shame, opposition, or the disapproval of others in society. Moral courage implies doing what is right even at the risk of inconvenience, scorn, castigation, loss of job, security or social status, etc. Moral courage calls for ethics and integrity and the fact that we resolve to match our words and action with values and ideals. It's not just about what we claim, but more about what we say and do. Moral courage necessitates that we rise above indifference, complacency, hate, pessimism, and fear-mongering in our political, economic, legal and social systems on the basis of differences or division.

Other scholars argue that courage can be divided into two; physical courage and moral courage. Physical courage is the courage to face hardship, physical pain and even the threat and possibility of death, while moral courage is the courage to face scandal, discouragement and even shame all in the name of doing what is morally right.[187] Moral courage includes the will to speak out and do what is right in the face of opposition that would lead us to act in some other way. Michael Woodford pointed out that, "if you know something is wrong and you choose to do nothing, you become complicit."[188] Moral courage is not keeping silent or keeping your head down when something is wrong; it is standing up to point out the wrong and trying to help correct it. The idea of being silent and meek in the face of injustice is common in Africa. The dangerous consequence of this attitude is exemplified by Martin Niemöller a prominent Lutheran pastor in Nazi Germany. He arose as an outspoken public adversary of Adolf Hitler and spent the last few years of Nazi rule in concentration camps. Niemöller is possibly immortalized by the quotation[189]: "First they came for the socialists, and I did not speak out—because I was not a socialist. Then they came for the trade unionists, and I did not speak out— because I was not a trade unionist. Then they came for the Jews, and I did not speak out— because I was not a Jew. Then they came for me—and there was no one left to speak for me."

If you do not speak out against injustices, poor governance and all the other things that cripple the country and the continent because of indifference or fear, one day you will find yourself at the center of it all and there will be nobody to speak for you. Even if you are

---

[187]Olsthoorn, P. (2007). Courage in the military: Physical and moral. Journal of Military Ethics, 6(4), 270-279.
[188]Burden, A. (2018, November 4). What is moral courage? Icas.Com. https://www.icas.com/members/professional-development/what-is-moral-courage
[189]Gerlach, W. (2000). And the Witnesses Were Silent: The Confessing Church and the Persecution of the Jews. U of Nebraska Press.

well off now and life is good for you, you need to speak for those who need a voice: you need to support those whose rights are being undermined. As Dr. Martin Luther King Jr wrote in 1963 when he was locked up in the Birmingham jail: "Injustice anywhere is a threat to justice everywhere. We are caught in an inescapable network of mutuality, tied in a single garment of destiny. Whatever affects one directly, affects all indirectly."[190] Your silence about the suffering of your country men and women will ultimately be you being silent on your own future, your children's fate and the destiny of your country and continent. Who will be left when they come for you in spite of the comfort or peace you have now? Moral courage says you need to do something about other people's plight when they are unjustly treated; you need to speak up when something is wrong, when the innocent is charged as guilty and the guilty roam free. You need to speak up.

Not everybody can claim to have moral courage, but it can be cultivated. Moral courage flourishes on empathy and compassion; the aptitude to understand the needs and hurts of others. The more you know someone, the more you care about them and the more you are willing to protect their interest. Having moral courage means you rise up and try to transform your society to make it a better place for you and others. To transform society, you need to excise moral courage in the seven spheres of society.

It is believed that society can be transformed through the

---

[190]King Jr, M. L. (1992). Letter from Birmingham jail. UC Davis L. Rev., 26, 835.

seven spheres of society, also known as the *seven spheres of influence*.[191] These spheres are thought to be the various dimensions of life that combine to make up society as we know it. Each sphere has a unique purpose and set of characteristics that set it apart. It is a fact that not everyone will agree with these definitions. However, as a means of gaining traction around the conversation of reforming society, there is a need to simplify the complexity of social issues. It is a belief that we all operate in more than one of the spheres and no one is restricted to a single sphere. The seven spheres' viewpoint is backed by the belief that each sphere has the capacity to positively or negatively influence society as a whole depending on the people who operate in those spheres. The spheres include:

- **Family**. Family is the building block of society. It is the place from where we get a sense of identity and it is where we learn our first lessons of values. Strong marriages can help develop strong families. Good parenting can help raise good citizens. In families, we can learn different things about life that can impact society. Parents need to take their obligations seriously and have to be selfless in the development of their children. They need to prepare their children for the uncertainty of the future. As parents teach your children the values of hard work, integrity, respect and the fact that they will grow and live in a world where people will have values that might contradict theirs. Instill in them the thirst to learn and grow to be a better

---

[191] Loren Cunningham, (Winning God's Way) YWAM Publishing 1988. Page 123

person. As parents be the example for your children, model the behavior you want them to possess; let your words match your actions. Broken relationships, abuse, a loss of identity, a sense of abandonment and an orphan mentality, communication break downs, rebellion, immorality and accusation are all evident in the family setting, but families can deliberately forge better, healthy and holistic qualities in their children. The truth is that the families people come from partly determine their success[192] and it has little to do with money but a lot to do with values, reputation and character. The family is the core of civilization and the basic social unit of society. For a civilization, continent, country or society to succeed, the family must succeed[193]. Broken families create broken people; broken people create broken societies.

- **Religion.** Despite the fact that religion is seen as an impediment in some societies, religion has significance in society. Religion assists in forming an ethical framework and also acts as a regulator for values in everyday life. It contributes to character building and acts as an agency of socialization. Religion contributes to structuring values like love, empathy, respect, and harmony

---

[192]Christenson, S. L., Rounds, T., & Gorney, D. (1992). Family factors and student achievement: An avenue to increase students' success. School Psychology Quarterly, 7(3), 178.
[193]Bennett, W. (2012, April 24). Stronger Families, Stronger Societies - NYTimes.com. The New York Times. https://www.nytimes.com/roomfordebate/2012/04/24/are-family-values-outdated/stronger-families-stronger-societies

which is important in any society. Religion strengthens family units, marriages, reduces poverty, helps in the formation of moral judgment, inoculates against social problems (such as drug abuse, suicide, crimes), and benefits personal physical help.[194]

- **Education**. Education is one of the most vital investments a country can make in its citizens and its future. Transformative education is very vital for the African society. A big part of the African education system is still stuck in the 1900s in a didactic pedagogy that limits a student's ability to critically think, be innovative and challenge their ability to learn. Quality education has the ability to transform society in a single generation due to the fact that it is a powerful agent of change, improves health and, livelihoods, contributes to social stability, and drives long-term economic growth. Quality education must instill character and values; it must create an intellect who is not just knowledgeable but also morally responsible. In the words of Stephen Covey: "As dangerous as a little knowledge is, even more dangerous is much knowledge without a strong, principled character. Purely intellectual development without commensurate internal character development makes as much sense as putting a high-powered sports car in the hands of a teenager who is high on drugs. Yet all too often in the academic world, that's exactly what we do by not focusing on the

---

194

character development of young people."[195] One of Africa's problems is that we have brilliant people who don't have a moral compass and the ones who do, don't use it. Our education systems have to create people who value and understand their obligation to society and not just to self. Formal education and knowledge for that matter is a privilege that not many have or can afford. Those who have it have the obligation to help others to attain it and harness the benefits of quality education.

- **Government.** In Africa, we need governments where justice and peace are protected and authority is used to serve the citizens not to violate their rights. We need public servants who serve and not those who rule over or abuse those who actually pay their salary. It is argued that the oldest and most basic justification for government is as a protector: protecting citizens from violence. When it comes to the role of government in society, the views vary and it has been and remains one of the most fundamental questions in all political discussions and debates. Some fundamental things are however essential and need to be provided for by a credible government. They can be categorized into three roles: protector, provider and investor.[196] The idea of government as protector necessitates

---

[195]Covey, S. R. (1992). Principle centered leadership. Simon and Schuster.
[196]Slaughter, A. (2017, February 13). 3 responsibilities every government has towards its citizens. World Economic Forum.
https://www.weforum.org/agenda/2017/02/government-responsibility-to-citizens-anne-marie-slaughter/

taxation to finance, train and equip a police force and an army; to construct courts houses and prisons; and to designate or elect the officials to forge and implement the laws citizens must comply with. The police are used internally for protection while the army addresses foreign threats by being able to meet and defend against other governments as well as to fight them if the need arises. The idea of government as provider implies that the government provides goods and services that individual citizens cannot provide for themselves. These goods and services can include infrastructure, such as roads, schools, hospitals; and the social welfare state that can cater to the vulnerable such as the elderly, disabled and unemployed. These allow citizens to thrive socially and economically, and thus deliver a social security that permits citizens to generate their own economic security. The idea of the government as an investor implies the need for the government to invest in a transformative education system, quality health services, inspire more active citizenship, and pursue binding international trade, cultural and collaborative alliances. This creates a national atmosphere that facilitates innovation, empowerment, creativity and collaboration which will transform Africa as a continent.

- **Economics (Science, Technology & Business).** When it comes to economics and the aspects of science and technology, Africa is way behind compared to other parts of the world but if integrity and determination is combined with the little we have, the story will be different. Africa is a wealthy continent when it comes to resources. The African economy is made up of trade, industry, agriculture, and human resources, with a population of over 1.3 billion people in 54 countries. Africa has all the makings of an economic giant. With the Covid-19 pandemic raging, the prospects are however bleak for Africa.[197] African governments need to enhance the economy by continuing to strengthen institutions, sustain political stability, promote democratization, improve policy coordination, enhance ease of doing business on the continent, reduce debt, open financial markets, attract authentic foreign direct investment, enable technology transfers, and cultivate human capital through education and health care[198]. Africa needs to nurture, educate and empower its young and vibrant population. We need to encourage and embrace local and indigenous innovations that allow us to develop our own solutions.

- **Celebration (Arts, Entertainment and Sports).** Celebration is the strengthening of hope and the building of a community through holistic presentations of life that engage the whole person. Arts and entertainment influences society by altering opinions, instilling values and translating

---

[197]World Bank. (2020, April 23). Overview. https://www.worldbank.org/en/region/afr/overview
[198]Coleman, C. (2020, February 11). The future of the African economy. World Economic Forum. https://www.weforum.org/agenda/2020/02/africa-global-growth-economics-worldwide-gdp/

experiences across space and time.[199] Art allows people from diverse cultures and different times to communicate with each other through images, sounds and stories. It also inspires us to value instinct, uncertainty, and inventiveness, and to continually search for new ideas. Similarly, sports create a sense of identity, unity and comradery. More specifically, sports are good for the mind, body and spirit;[200] team sports in particular teach youths responsibility, commitment, leadership, as well as other skills. When done well, arts, entertainment and sports can transform social mindsets and create new perspectives on how things should be done. For example, in many parts of Africa, people believe that being "sharp" is a good thing. It implies street smart and the ability to navigate shady situations and so when public funds are stolen or mismanaged, the perpetrators are labelled as "sharp". This suggests that to succeed, a person needs to be sharp, and needs to know how to break the law without getting caught. This mindset is of course flawed, and arts, entertainment and sport can change such in societies through role models who embody the ideals that can better society. It is also a tragedy that most African parents do not want their

---

[199]Rabang, I. (2020, March 20). Art and Its Impact on Society: Art Districts Revitalizing Communities. Bold Business.
https://www.boldbusiness.com/society/art-and-its-impact-on-society-art-districts-revitalizing-communities/
[200]Eigenschenk, B., Thomann, A., McClure, M., Davies, L., Gregory, M., Dettweiler, U., & Inglés, E. (2019). Benefits of outdoor sports for society. A systematic literature review and reflections on evidence. International journal of environmental research and public health, 16(6), 937.

children to go into the creative arts, entertainment or sports[201]. They only want their children to go into Medicine, Law, Finance, or Engineering regardless of where their true talents rest[202]. Now we know that some of the most successful and celebrated Africans are in the creative arts, entertainment and sports. It is therefore important to know that a person operating in their talent and passion will never work a day in their life and their drive will always create wealth and repute. That is the law of nature. We have enough doctors, lawyers and engineers who don't have the passion for their profession. They are doing it purely for the money and are unwilling to be creative, challenge themselves and go the extra mile. In other cases, these professionals are poorly paid and they seek better opportunities elsewhere resulting in brain drain[203] for the lucky few and a great loss for the continent[204]. I am not saying other fields are not important; I am saying that the creative arts, entertainments and sports are also very important and can make an immense contribution to society[205].

---

[201] Smith-Walters, M. (2019, April 27). "African parents don't see creative jobs as a career." BBC News. https://www.bbc.com/news/av/world-africa-48058193
[202] Adamu, J. (2018, May 30). Growing Up African. Medium. https://medium.com/@josefadamu/growing-up-african-2018-9b6d5a9aba2b
[203] Gwaradzimba, E., & Shumba, A. (2010). The nature, extent and impact of the brain drain in Zimbabwe and South Africa. Acta Academica, 42(1), 209-241.
[204] Benedict, S. O. H., & Ukpere, W. I. (2013). Brain drain and African development: Any possible gain from the drain?. African Journal of Business Management, 6(7), 2421-2428
[205] Snowball, J. (2016, January 21). How much does art and culture contribute to economic growth? World Economic Forum. https://www.weforum.org/agenda/2016/01/how-much-does-art-and-culture-contribute-to-economic-growth

- **Media**. The media influences us extensively, both consciously and subconsciously. This includes mass media and social media. The media we consume influences our perception of the world, how it works and how we should react to it[206]. This makes the media perhaps one of the most powerful influences in human life. Over the years, the western media has portrayed Africa in an unflattering light and has fueled the perception of Africa being backward, poverty-riddled and completely unsafe[207]. It is not uncommon to see some Hollywood movies and sometimes western journalists in the recent past portray an African city like Lagos as a village with lions roaming around the poverty-stricken huts[208]. The media influences our values, cultures, beliefs and self-worth, and continues to do so for good or bad. Sadly, in the case of Africa, western media tends to be negative from the poverty-stricken cities in the news to the African character in the Hollywood movies dying first (possibly by the hand or in the hands of a white protagonist)[209]. The general effect of mass media has risen radically over the years

---

[206] Happer, C., & Philo, G. (2013). The role of the media in the construction of public belief and social change. Journal of social and political psychology, 1(1), 321-336.

[207] Schraeder, P. J., & Endless, B. (1998). The Media and Africa: The Portrayal of Africa in the" New York Times"(1955-1995). Issue: A Journal of Opinion, 26(2), 29-35.

[208] Ukadike, N. F. (1990). Western film images of Africa: Genealogy of an ideological formulation. The Black Scholar, 21(2), 30-48.

[209] Njambi, W. N., & O'Brien, W. E. (2018). Hollywood's Africa: Lessons in race, gender, and stereotype. Review of Education, Pedagogy, and Cultural Studies, 40(4), 349-366.

and will continue to do so as the media evolves and continues to influence our perception.[210] These influences range from the positive such as education and enlightenment to the negative such as inciting violence and false information. However, by deliberately using one's influence in the media to create a positive impact, society can always benefit. This can be done by everyone from social media[211] usage to reporters[212] being truthful, honest and fair in the portrayal of the news and of the continent.

True courage is the willingness to dare to make a difference in the spheres of influence you operate in. Courage is like a muscle that needs training, discipline, and plenty of opportunities for practice. Moral courage may sound like a lofty idea but it is actually a simple and achievable quality. We can all exercise it in our everyday life by doing what is right not because of what we expect to gain for ourselves but for what we hope to gain for our children, our contemporaries, our generation, our future and our country. True courage is speaking up and doing what is right because it is the right thing to do.

---

[210] Valkenburg, P. M., Peter, J., & Walther, J. B. (2016). Media effects: Theory and research. Annual review of psychology, 67, 315-338.
[211] Ortiz-Ospina, E. (2019). The rise of social media. Our World in Data, 18.
[212] Kahn, K. F., & Kenney, P. J. (2002). The slant of the news: How editorial endorsements influence campaign coverage and citizens' views of candidates. American political science review, 96(2), 381-394.

THE INTEGRITY CLAUSE

Conclusion

"As I have said, the first thing is to be honest with yourself. You can never have an impact on society if you have not changed yourself. Great peacemakers are all people of integrity, of honesty, but humility."
Nelson Mandela

"Your pride for your country should not come after your country becomes great; your country becomes great because of your pride in it."
Idowu Koyenikan

"If we don't kill corruption, corruption will kill us."
Muhammadu Buhari

When all is said and done, the world has never been changed by ideals and well-wishers. It has been changed by people who take action and do the little they can to make a difference. Human societies have always been defined by the few individuals who choose to do something. Sadly, it can be for good or bad. It is very easy to have a negative influence on society and we have a lot of examples of that on the African continent. To do something remarkable calls for commitment, honesty, humility and perhaps most importantly integrity.

It is important to understand that corruption undermines the legitimacy of any government. It destroys people's lives and practically enslaves even the most talented and gifted. Corruption increases transaction costs and creates insecurity in the economy by obstructing foreign and domestic investments and frustrates fledging talents due to income and distorted sectorial priorities[213]. Corruption farther deteriorates the state's capacity to grow revenue and results into ever-increasing tax rates due to the fact that the few who actually pay taxes are overburdened. It simply leads to the imposition of regressive taxes on commercial and service activities performed by businesses. Consequently, lessening the state's ability to provide enough public goods, including the rule of law[214].

We know that corruption is everywhere and is a result of a cocktail of factors such as the political and economic setting, professional standards and laws, as well as

---

[213] Tanzi, V., & Davoodi, H. (1997). Corruption, public investment, and growth (IMF Working Paper, 97/139). International Monetary Fund, Washington DC.
[214] Kaufmann, D& Gray CW. (1998). Corruption and development. Finance & Development, 35(1):7

factors, such as customs, habits and traditions. According to Svensson,[215] the most corrupt countries in the world are characterized by being in the developing world, low-income countries, have a closed economy, the influence of religion is visible, low media freedom and low levels of education. In the long run, corruption destroys everything; even its benefactors.

Interestingly, studies[216] have confirmed the effects of reduced corruption on a country and how it can transform the GDP per capita and the average per capita income. In simple terms, reduction of corruption reduces poverty. To overcome the devastation of corruption and to redeem the African continent from its destitution, integrity is needed. Integrity is a personal choice[217].

I cannot guarantee you that integrity will make you wealthy or famous but integrity will surely make your life worth living and it will make others' lives worth living because you have integrity. Just look at your environment, where you live, work or go to school and try to identify some problems that exist there. When you look at it long enough and close enough, you might find that the root cause is a result of the lack of integrity. I personally believe that integrity is the pillar that holds up modern and thriving societies. If there is no integrity at

---

[215] Svensson, J. (2005). Eight questions about corruption. Journal of economic perspectives, 19(3), 19-42.
[216] Wei SJ. Corruption in Economic Transition and Development: Grease or Sand? Geneva: United Nations Economic Commission for Europe; 2001
[217] Whitfield, E. (2018, April 12). How Can We Reduce Corruption if Integrity is a Personal Choice? Chemonics International. https://www.chemonics.com/blog/how-can-we-reduce-corruption-if-integrity-is-a-personal-choice/

all, nothing will work: the house you live in will collapse, the education you acquire will be regressive, the job you work in will be exploitative and everything you hold dear might not turn out to be what you expected it to be.

In spite of the belief of some societies that you have to be "sharp", integrity is a long-term game and a sustainable one. Being dishonest can take you places but in time it will fail because the truth always prevails and hard work and determination always speak for themselves. It is a common saying that talent, knowledge, networks and opportunities can take you places but its integrity that can keep you there. The collapse of empires, nations and powerful people have been due to the failure of integrity in their past or their present. Integrity protects, it builds and it transforms.

It is my understanding that true knowledge influences behaviour and our behaviour is a result of how we choose to respond to what is around or before us. I hope this book will inspire you to be a better person, a better African, and a positive influence for change in your society. I pray this book will make you want to reach for more than yourself, fight for social justice and see beyond the present into the future. I desire that this book will make you see what a legacy you can create among your contemporaries and for the future of the great continent of Africa. You don't have to be African to make this change, you don't have to live in Africa to make this change and you don't have to move mountains to help Africa become a better place for all humanity. You just need to choose to exercise integrity; to be true and stand for what is right and just. Nothing great is achieved without integrity. And every great movement or revolution starts with one person who inspires others to join and change the world. We are all leaders and influencers in our respective spheres of influence; our integrity takes us to another level to effect positive change. Be it big or small. To make one person's life better and worth living is to make their children and their children's children's life that much better. It can always have a knock-on effect.

It is indeed time to activate the integrity clause: the pledge to commit to practice integrity in all your undertaking in spite of the temptation and the impossibilities. To have an impact, you have to act; to act, you need to have integrity, otherwise, you might be part of the problem. A problem that might come back to haunt you, your children and your children's children.

ABOUT THE AUTHOR

Olutayo K. Osunsan was born in Lagos, Nigeria and he lives in Kampala, Uganda with his wife and children. When he is not writing, he works as a lecturer in Business Management. He is the author of several books including *Strange Beauty* (2004), *The Poet in May* (2006), *The Life of One* (2010), *The Alchemy of Butterfly Memories* (2011), *The Life of Another One* (2013), *Business Communications* (2014), *This Happiness* (2015), *Leo* (2019), and *Internationalizing Growth* (2020). Olutayo's poems have appeared in several publications and websites on four continents. A few of his poems have been translated into foreign languages such as Chinese and German. Olutayo's writings express his faith in God, his love for the African continent, the inner turmoil of everyday people and the struggle to rise above imperfection.

Made in the USA
Columbia, SC
10 November 2024